SELECTED POEMS OF RAINER MARIA RILKE

Other Books by Robert Bly

POETRY

Silence in the Snowy Fields
The Light Around the Body
The Teeth Mother Naked at Last
Jumping Out of Bed
Sleepers Joining Hands
Old Man Rubbing His Eyes
The Morning Glory
This Body Is Made of Camphor and Gopherwood
This Tree Will Be Here for a Thousand Years

TRANSLATIONS (POETRY)

Twenty Poems of Georg Trakl
        (with James Wright)
Neruda and Vallejo: Selected Poems
        (with James Wright and John Knoepfle)
Lorca and Jimenez: Selected Poems
Friends, You Drank Some Darkness. Martinson, Ekelof
        and Transtromer: Selected Poems
Basho: Twelve Poems
The Kabir Book: 44 of the Ecstatic Poems of Kabir
Twenty Poems of Rolf Jacobsen
Mirabai: Six Versions

TRANSLATIONS (FICTION)

Hunger by Knut Hamsun
The Story of Gosta Berling by Selma Lagerlöf

INTERVIEWS

Talking All Morning: Collected Interviews and Conversations

ANTHOLOGIES

News of the Universe: Poems of Twofold Consciousness

Selected Poems of

RAINER MARIA RILKE

A Translation from the German and Commentary by Robert Bly

1817

PERENNIAL LIBRARY

Harper & Row, Publishers, New York
Grand Rapids, Philadelphia, St. Louis, San Francisco
London, Singapore, Sydney, Tokyo, Toronto

Many friends have helped over years with these translations, and I want especially to thank Lisel Mueller, Donald Hall, Saul Galin and James Scherer.

I am grateful to the editors of the following magazines or smaller editions who have published some of these poems: *Dacotah Territory, Doones, Hoof and Mouth, Michigan Quarterly Review, The Minnesota Review, Parabola, Plainsong,* and *Roadapple Review.*

The ten *Voices* were printed as a booklet by Alby Press. The first ten *Stundenbuch* poems appeared as "I Am Too Alone in the World," published by the Silver Hands Press; "Archaic Torso of Apollo" appeared as a broadside by James Hartz.

Designed by Sidney Feinberg

Library of Congress Cataloging in Publication Data

Rilke, Rainer Maria, 1875–1926.
    Selected poems of Rainer Maria Rilke.
    English and German.
    Includes indexes.
    I. Bly, Robert. II. Title.
PT2635.I65A23   1979   831'.9'12   79–2114
ISBN 0–06–010432–5
ISBN 0–06–090727–4 (pbk.)

91 92 93 94 CC/FG   14 15 16 17 18 19 20

Contents

FROM The Book of Pictures
Das Buch der Bilder

———

FROM The Uncollected
and Occasional Poems

FROM Sonnets to Orpheus
Die Sonette an Orpheus

FROM A Book for the Hours of Prayer

(*Das Stundenbuch*)

1899–1903

RILKE'S FIRST LARGE BOOK, and the first he had confidence in, was *Das Stundenbuch*, which I have translated as *A Book for the Hours of Prayer*. The German title suggests a medieval monk's or nun's handbook of prayers. *Innigkeit* is the German word associated with such poetry, which becomes "inwardness" in English; but the syllables of the German word have so much more drive and finality than the English sounds. *Innigkeit* has the depth of a well where one finds water. And water is the element of this book, a water whose source Rilke found inside himself.

The first group of poems in the book, called "The Book of Monkish Life," came in a wonderful rush, shortly after Rilke returned home from a trip to Russia with Lou Andreas-Salomé and her husband in 1899. He was twenty-three years old. Until then he had felt his life to be constricted and restrained: the narrow streets of his native Prague seemed stiflingly provincial, and his mother's love and her piety left little space for him. He later said of her:

> *In some heart-attic she is tucked away*
> *and Christ comes there to wash her every day.*

The power of Lou Andreas-Salomé's personality and the open spaces of the Russian plains astounded him. He understood Russia's outer space as inner space. It lay east of "Europe":

> *Sometimes a man stands up during supper*
> *and walks outdoors, and keeps on walking,*
> *because of a church that stands somewhere in the East.*
>
> *And his children say blessings on him as if he were dead.*
>
> *And another man, who remains inside his own house,*
> *stays there, inside the dishes and in the glasses,*
> *so that his children have to go far out into the world*
> *toward that same church, which he forgot.*

He doesn't mean any orthodox church, but says that if a man walks toward that inner space, he will free his children. It is not too late.

> *Because One Man wanted so much to have you,*
> *I know that we can all want you.*

He is astonished to realize that this wanting and having are perfectly possible right now, even for twentieth-century man. Growth is growth into space, as a tree grows through its rings, as the snail grows in spirals and the solar system moves in circles:

> *I live my life in growing orbits*
> *which move out over the things of the world.*
> *Perhaps I can never achieve the last,*
> *but that will be my attempt.*
>
> *I am circling around God, around the ancient tower,*
> *and I have been circling for a thousand years,*
> *and I still don't know if I am a falcon, or a storm,*
> *or a great song.*

In his surprise he doesn't even identify himself as a man; he could be a falcon or a storm.

Before his Russian trip, Rilke had spent a few months in Italy, and he loved the religious paintings of the early Renaissance, the heavy gold frames, the gold flake: he noticed that the Mediterranean psyche associated gold with religious feeling. But he saw something different when he looked within himself— what we could call a North European unconscious.

> *I have many brothers in the South.*
> *Laurels stand there in monastery gardens.*
> *I know in what a human way they imagine the Madonna,*
> *and I think often of young Titians*
> *through whom God walks burning.*
>
> *Yet no matter how deeply I go down into myself*
> *my God is dark, and like a webbing made*
> *of a hundred roots, that drink in silence.*

He then realizes that he may have claimed too much for himself, and he delicately suggests how unformed he is:

I know that my trunk rose from his warmth, but that's all,
because my branches hardly move at all
near the ground, and only wave a little in the wind.

The language broods; it stays in the moist mood of the North
European unconscious. The holy is below us, not above; and a
line moves to descend, to dip down, to touch water that lies so
near we are astonished our hands haven't dipped into it before.
The lines suggest holy depth, always distant, always close.

> *I love the dark hours of my being*
> *in which my senses drop into the deep.*

He becomes aware that he has two separate lives.

> *My life is not this steeply sloping hour,*
> *in which you see me hurrying. . . .*
> *I am only one of my many mouths,*
> *and at that the one that will be still the soonest.*

He loves the tension between the poles, hurry and quiet, life
and death. Even though death's note wants to dominate, he is
the rest between two notes:

> *. . . in the dark interval, reconciled,*
> *—they stay there trembling.*
> *And the song goes on, beautiful.*

The problem is not whether the song will continue, but whether
a dark space can be found where the notes can resonate. This
dark space resembles the hub of a wheel, a pitcher, the hold of
a ship that carries us "through the wildest storm of all," the
grave earth under the tree, the lower branches of a pine, the
darkness at the edge of a bonfire. The dark space is the water
in the well. This hub, or hold, or dark space, is not a Pre-Raphaelite
preciosity, nor the light of narcissism; the dark space can be
rough and dangerous. It is something out there, with the energy
of an animal, and at the same instant it is far inside. Once a
man or a woman inhabits that space, he or she finds it hidden
inside objects, in walnuts or tree roots, in places where people
don't ordinarily look for it.

I find you in all these things of the world
that I love calmly, like a brother;
in things no one cares for you brood like a seed;
and to powerful things you give an immense power.

Strength plays such a marvelous game—
it moves through the things of the world like a servant,
groping out in roots, tapering in trunks,
and in the treetops like a rising from the dead.

How magnificent the last line is! In German: *"und in den Wipfeln wie ein Auferstehn."* This "darkness" or "hub" or "circling power" is a strength best discovered in objects. The word Rilke loves, *Ding*, literally "thing," is difficult. Of course, he means "things" and "objects" by it, but also animals, and even thunder and rocks. "Things of the world" is a attempt to include what he includes in it. He notices that the energy takes the shape and mood of the creature it is in—when it roots, it gropes; when it trunks, it tapers.

A Book for the Hours of Prayer circles, then, with an athletic power inside inner space, among secret things.

and in the silent, sometimes hardly moving times
when something is coming near,
I want to be with those who know secret things
or else alone.

It can be a shock for readers used to public literature. Most American writers begin proudly, even aggressively, in the outer world: Thoreau, Mark Twain, Howells, Robinson Jeffers, Marianne Moore, Robert Frost, the Eliot who listened to conversations in bars, the William Carlos Williams who paid attention to back sheds and wheelbarrows. Their start in the outer world is marvelous, but Rilke begins elsewhere. When I first read Rilke, in my twenties, I felt a deep shock upon realizing the amount of introversion he had achieved, and the adult attention he paid to inner states. From the pragmatist or objectivist point of view, Rilke goes too far in this attention; he goes over the line. The American, in Latin America or North America, is willing to accept some introversion, but when it goes this far, he may dismiss the whole thing as solipsism, or as an evasion of political responsibility. Neruda attacked Rilke on precisely this point, in "Poetes Celestes," though late in his life he took back the criticism.

Rilke knows what Tolstoy knows in *The Death of Ivan Ilyich:* that our day-by-day life, with its patterns and familiar objects, can become a husk that blocks anything fresh from coming in. Before the industrial revolution brought its various creature comforts, it is conceivable that the shocks of winter cold, sudden poverties, plague, brutal invasions, abrupt unexplainable deaths, regularly broke the husk. In our time the husk is strong, and Rilke turns to look at it. A man or woman inside the husk, Rilke says, resembles a medieval city that has succeeded—so far—in withstanding or ignoring a siege.

> *All of you undisturbed cities,*
> *haven't you ever longed for the Enemy?*

The fairy tale called "Sleeping Beauty" describes this situation of invisible siege, where the woman—and perhaps the soul—sleeps undisturbed inside a wall of thorns. No one can get through. In the fairy tale, the "man" or the "suitor" is the awakening force, who fails again and again; the Sufis interpret the last suitor as the spiritual teacher or master. In Rilke's poem the awakening force is a massive energy *out there,* symbolized by an encamped army and the countryside itself.

> *He lies outside the walls like a countryside. . . .*
> *Climb up on your roofs and look out:*
> *his camp is there, and his morale doesn't falter,*
> *his numbers do not decrease, he will not grow weaker,*
> *and he sends no one into the city to threaten*
> *or promise, and no one to negotiate.*

When I translated the last few lines, I felt frightened; the lines imply that the awakening force will not make the first move; perhaps no one will come to help, no parents, no gurus, no Christ. When the walls break, Rilke says, they break "in silence."

When the walls are broken, the energy approaches.

and in the silent, sometimes hardly moving times
when something is coming near,
I want to be with those who know secret things
or else alone.

Realizing that the energy that tapers in trunks and gropes in roots can be met or touched, Rilke begins to speak of that energy as "you." Sometimes the "you" is the dark space I've mentioned, inhabiting the hold or the pitcher:

You darkness, that I come from,
I love you more than all the fires
that fence in the world . . .

Sometimes the "you" is a primitive initiatory force, female in tone:

you are the early dawn, from whom the whole
morning rose . . .

At other times it is the inner guide, a Khadir or "Faithful John"; at yet other times it is the collective "God" in his more conventional role.

And if that is arrogance, then I will stay arrogant
for the sake of my prayer
that is so sincere and solitary
standing before your cloudy forehead.

When he speaks of it as "deltas," or when he says

. . . your primitive wind is blowing
the fragrance of your marvelous power
to every being and to every creature in need

We sense it is related to the primitive uprushing of non-ego waters that Freud called "the unconscious." Freud published *The Interpretation of Dreams* in 1899, the same year Rilke wrote the first group of these poems. Rilke does not insist on any one identification of the "you," nor does he insist that he is always active. In one energetic and sweet poem, he describes himself

as no more active than a watchman in the wine fields, who stays
in a shed at night to keep robbers away.

> *odor pours out from your heavy boughs,*
> *and you never ask if I am keeping watch or not;*
> *confident, dissolved by the juices, your depths*
> *keep climbing past me silently.*

In *A Book for the Hours of Prayer* Rilke included three separate
groups of poems, written in different places at different times.
The second group, which he called "The Book of Pilgrimage,"
was written two years after his return from Russia. A selection
from that group begins here with poem number 18. He had moved
to an artists' colony called Worpswede, near Bremen, in a moor-
like country, and was living among landscape painters. We notice
in Rilke's creative life, as in Yeats's and Mallarmé's, the cross-
fertilization between poetry and painting; in Rilke's case, between
poetry and sculpture as well. The two painters Heinrich Vogeler
and Otto Modersohn became close friends of Rilke's at Worps-
wede; Rilke was probably in love with both Paula Becker and
Clara Westhoff. He loved Paula Becker deeply but she married
Otto Modersohn, and it was Clara, a sculptor of great ability,
whom Rilke married.

The sense of "the road" continues in "The Book of Pilgrim-
age"; the sense of danger also increases. Rilke sees that it is
possible to "die on the road" if you leave the conventional warmth
of collectivized feeling.

> *The tiny town is only a passing-over place,*
> *worried and afraid, between two huge spaces. . . .*
>
> *And those who leave the town wander a long way off*
> *and many perhaps die on the road.*

During this time he wrote "Already the ripening barberries are
red," his marvelous poem on fall. In fall Rilke always tried to
give himself time alone to look within; in the fall, he found, one
can look down long avenues of trees inside, when the vision is
not blocked by leaves.

Already the ripening barberries are red,
and the old asters hardly breathe in their beds.
The man who is not rich now as summer goes
will wait and wait and never be himself.

The test of whether you owned yourself was this: to close the eyes, and wait to see what sort of images rose up around you in the dark.

The man who cannot quietly close his eyes,
certain that there is vision after vision
inside, simply waiting until nighttime
to rise all around him in the darkness—
it's all over for him, he's like an old man.

The danger is greatest for those who have started on the road. If the psychic power is then dissipated by sociability or dishonesty or triviality, the man or woman is in danger.

Nothing else will come; no more days will open,
and everything that does happen will cheat him.
Even you, my God. And you are like a stone
that draws him daily deeper into the depths.

God himself is dangerous. These lines mark the first appearance of this idea, which will later dominate the Second Elegy.

Rilke named the last group of poems "The Book of Poverty and Death," and a selection from that group begins here with poem number 22. By that time two more years had passed; Clara and he had married, and their daughter, Ruth, had been born. Supporting a family at Worpswede was impossible, and he and Clara decided he should accept a commission on a prose piece and move to Paris. He wrote the third set of poems in a rush, at Viareggio, but they came after his first experience of a great modern city, of Paris.

And the great cities, Lord, what are they?
Places disintegrating and abandoned.
The city I know resembles animals fleeing from a fire.
The shelter it gave has no shelter now,
and the age of the cities is nearly over.

Neither writing nor living was easy.

> *It's possible I am pushing through solid rock*
> *in flintlike layers, as the ore lies, alone;*
> *I am such a long way in I see no way through,*
> *and no space: everything is close to my face,*
> *and everything close to my face is stone.*

Saint Francis, whom he loved, had praised poverty; but the idea didn't seem useful to the poor in Paris.

> *And where is he, the clear one, whose tone rings to us?*
> *Why don't the poor feel him, the rejoicing one,*
> *mastering us, the young one, even though far off?*

> *Why doesn't he climb then in their dusk—*
> *the great evening star of poverty.*

Rilke in Paris, then, began to experience a poverty that does not necessarily lead to spirit; and his tremendous energy turned to face that dark.

Ich lebe mein Leben in wachsenden Ringen,
die sich über die Dinge ziehn.
Ich werde den letzten vielleicht nicht vollbringen,
aber versuchen will ich ihn.

Ich kreise um Gott, um den uralten Turm,
und ich kreise jahrtausendelang;
und ich weiss noch nicht: bin ich ein Falke, ein Sturm
oder ein grosser Gesang.

1

I live my life in growing orbits
which move out over the things of the world.
Perhaps I can never achieve the last,
but that will be my attempt.

I am circling around God, around the ancient tower,
and I have been circling for a thousand years,
and I still don't know if I am a falcon, or a storm,
or a great song.

Ich habe viele Brüder in Sutanen
im Süden, wo in Klöstern Lorbeer steht.
Ich weiss, wie menschlich sie Madonnen planen,
und träume oft von jungen Tizianen,
durch die der Gott in Gluten geht.

Doch wie ich mich auch in mich selber neige:
Mein Gott ist dunkel und wie ein Gewebe
von hundert Wurzeln, welche schweigsam trinken.
Nur, dass ich mich aus seiner Wärme hebe,
mehr weiss ich nicht, weil alle meine Zweige
tief unten ruhn und nur im Winde winken.

2

I have many brothers in the South.
Laurels stand there in monastery gardens.
I know in what a human way they imagine the Madonna,
and I think often of young Titians
through whom God walks burning.

Yet no matter how deeply I go down into myself
my God is dark, and like a webbing made
of a hundred roots, that drink in silence.
I know that my trunk rose from his warmth, but that's all,
because my branches hardly move at all
near the ground, and just wave a little in the wind.

Wir dürfen dich nicht eigenmächtig malen,
du Dämmernde, aus der der Morgen stieg.
Wir holen aus den alten Farbenschalen
die gleichen Striche und die gleichen Strahlen,
mit denen dich der Heilige verschwieg.

Wir bauen Bilder vor dir auf wie Wände;
so dass schon tausend Mauern um dich stehn.
Denn dich verhüllen unsre frommen Hände,
sooft dich unsre Herzen offen sehn.

3

We don't dare to do paintings of you as we want to:
you are the early dawn, from whom the whole morning rose.
We haul out of the ancient color boxes
the same strokes and the same brilliant light
with which the Great Saint kept you secret.

We construct paintings all around you like walls,
so that thousands of walls are standing around you now.
Our pious hands lay a cover over you
whenever we feel that you are open toward us.

Ich liebe meines Wesens Dunkelstunden,
in welchen meine Sinne sich vertiefen;
in ihnen hab ich, wie in alten Briefen,
mein täglich Leben schon gelebt gefunden
und wie Legende weit und uberwunden.
Aus ihnen kommt mir Wissen, dass ich Raum
zu einem zweiten zeitlos breiten Leben habe.

Und manchmal bin ich wie der Baum,
der, reif und rauschend, über einem Grabe
den Traum erfüllt, den der vergangne Knabe
(um den sich seine warmen Wurzeln drängen)
verlor in Traurigkeiten und Gesängen.

4

I love the dark hours of my being
in which my senses drop into the deep.
I have found in them, as in old letters,
my private life, that is already lived through,
and become wide and powerful now, like legends.
Then I know that there is room in me
for a second huge and timeless life.

But sometimes I am like the tree that stands
over a grave, a leafy tree, fully grown,
who has lived out that particular dream, that the dead boy
(around whom its warm roots are pressing)
lost through his sad moods and his poems.

Du Dunkelheit, aus der ich stamme,
ich liebe dich mehr als die Flamme,
welche die Welt begrenzt,
indem sie glänzt
für irgend einen Kreis,
aus dem heraus kein Wesen von ihr weiss.

Aber die Dunkelheit hält alles an sich:
Gestalten und Flammen, Tiere und mich,
wie sie's errafft,
Menschen und Mächte—

Und es kann sein: eine grosse Kraft
rührt sich in meiner Nachbarschaft.

Ich glaube an Nächte.

5

You darkness, that I come from,
I love you more than all the fires
that fence in the world,
for the fire makes
a circle of light for everyone,
and then no one outside learns of you.

But the darkness pulls in everything:
shapes and fires, animals and myself,
how easily it gathers them!—
powers and people—

and it is possible a great energy
is moving near me.

I have faith in nights.

Ich glaube an alles noch nie Gesagte.
Ich will meine frömmsten Gefühle befrein.
Was noch keiner zu wollen wagte,
wird mir einmal unwillkürlich sein.

Ist das vermessen, mein Gott, vergib.
Aber ich will dir damit nur sagen:
Meine beste Kraft soll sein wie ein Trieb,
so ohne Zürnen und ohne Zagen;
so haben dich ja die Kinder lieb.

Mit diesem Hinfluten, mit diesem Münden
in breiten Armen ins offene Meer,
mit dieser wachsenden Wiederkehr
will ich dich bekennen, will ich dich verkünden
wie keiner vorher.

Und ist das Hoffahrt, so lass mich hoffährtig sein
für mein Gebet,
das so ernst und allein
vor deiner wolkigen Stirne steht.

6

I have faith in all those things that are not yet said.
I want to set free my most holy feelings.
What no one has dared to want
will be for me impossible to refuse.

If that is presumption, then, my God, forgive me.
However, I want to tell you this one thing:
I want my best strength to be like a shoot,
with no anger and no timidity, as a shoot is;
this is the way the children love you.

With these ebbing tides, with these mouths
opening their deltas into the open sea,
with these returns, that keep growing,
I want to acknowledge you, I want to announce you,
as no one ever has before.

And if that is arrogance, then I will stay arrogant
for the sake of my prayer,
that is so sincere and solitary
standing before your cloudy forehead.

Ich bin auf der Welt zu allein und doch nicht allein genug,
um jede Stunde zu weihn.
Ich bin auf der Welt zu gering und doch nicht klein genug,
um vor dir zu sein wie ein Ding,
dunkel und klug.
Ich will meinen Willen und will meinen Willen begleiten
die Wege zur Tat;
und will in stillen, irgendwie zögernden Zeiten,
wenn etwas naht,
unter den Wissenden sein
oder allein.
Ich will dich immer spiegeln in ganzer Gestalt,
und will niemals blind sein oder zu alt,
um dein schweres schwankendes Bild zu halten.
Ich will mich entfalten.
Nirgends will ich gebogen bleiben,
denn dort bin ich gelogen, wo ich gebogen bin.
Und ich will meinen Sinn
wahr vor dir. Ich will mich beschreiben
wie ein Bild, das ich sah,
lange und nah,
wie ein Wort, das ich begriff,
wie meinen täglichen Krug,
wie meiner Mutter Gesicht,
wie ein Schiff,
das mich trug
durch den tödlichsten Sturm.

7

I am too alone in the world, and not alone enough
to make every minute holy.
I am too tiny in this world, and not tiny enough
just to lie before you like a thing,
shrewd and secretive.
I want my own will, and I want simply to be with my will,
as it goes toward action,
and in the silent, sometimes hardly moving times
when something is coming near,
I want to be with those who know secret things
or else alone.
I want to be a mirror for your whole body,
and I never want to be blind, or to be too old
to hold up your heavy and swaying picture.
I want to unfold.
I don't want to stay folded anywhere,
because where I am folded, there I am a lie.
And I want my grasp of things
true before you. I want to describe myself
like a painting that I looked at
closely for a long time,
like a saying that I finally understood,
like the pitcher I use every day,
like the face of my mother,
like a ship
that took me safely
through the wildest storm of all.

Du siehest, ich will viel.
Vielleicht will ich Alles:
das Dunkel jedes unendlichen Falles
und jedes Steigens lichtzitterndes Spiel.

Es leben so viele und wollen nichts,
und sind durch ihres leichten Gerichts
glatte Gefühle gefurstet.

Aber du freust dich jedes Gesichts,
das dient und dürstet.

Du freust dich aller, die dich gebrauchen
wie ein Gerät.

Noch bist du nicht kalt, und es ist nicht zu spät,
in deine werdenden Tiefen zu tauchen,
wo sich das Leben ruhig verrät.

8

You see, I want a lot.
Perhaps I want everything:
the darkness that comes with every infinite fall
and the shivering blaze of every step up.

So many live on and want nothing,
and are raised to the rank of prince
by the slippery ease of their light judgments.

But what you love to see are faces
that do work and feel thirst.

You love most of all those who need you
as they need a crowbar or a hoe.

You have not grown old, and it is not too late
to dive into your increasing depths
where life calmly gives out its own secret.

Daraus, dass Einer dich einmal gewollt hat,
weiss ich, dass wir dich wollen dürfen.
Wenn wir auch alle Tiefen verwürfen:
wenn ein Gebirge Gold hat
und keiner mehr es ergraben mag,
trägt es einmal der Fluss zutag,
der in die Stille der Steine greift,
der vollen.

Auch wenn wir nicht wollen:

Gott reift.

9

Because One Man wanted so much to have you,
I know that we can all want you.
Even when we throw all depths away from us:
suppose a mountain has gold
and no one is allowed to mine it anymore;
the water will bring it to light, the water
which reaches into the silence of stone,
it does the wanting.

Even when we do not use our will:

God is growing.

Mein Leben ist nicht diese steile Stunde,
darin du mich so eilen siehst.
Ich bin ein Baum vor meinem Hintergrunde,
ich bin nur einer meiner vielen Munde
und jener, welcher sich am frühsten schliesst.

Ich bin die Ruhe zwischen zweien Tönen,
die sich nur schlecht aneinander gewöhnen:
denn der Ton Tod will sich erhöhn—
Aber im dunklen Intervall versöhnen
sich beide zitternd.
                        Und das Lied bleibt schön.

10

My life is not this steeply sloping hour,
in which you see me hurrying.
Much stands behind me; I stand before it like a tree;
I am only one of my many mouths,
and at that, the one that will be still the soonest.

I am the rest between two notes,
which are somehow always in discord
because Death's note wants to climb over—
but in the dark interval, reconciled,
they stay there trembling.
                    And the song goes on, beautiful.

Ich finde dich in allen diesen Dingen,
denen ich gut und wie ein Bruder bin;
als Samen sonnst du dich in den geringen
und in den grossen gibst du gross dich hin.

Das ist das wundersame Spiel der Kräfte,
dass sie so dienend durch die Dinge gehn:
in Wurzeln wachsend, schwindend in die Schäfte
und in den Wipfeln wie ein Auferstehn.

11

I find you in all these things of the world
that I love calmly, like a brother;
in things no one cares for you brood like a seed;
and to powerful things you give an immense power.

Strength plays such a marvelous game—
it moves through the things of the world like a servant,
groping out in roots, tapering in trunks,
and in the treetops like a rising from the dead.

Da ward auch die zur Frucht Erweckte,
die schüchterne und schönerschreckte,
die heimgesuchte Magd geliebt.
Die Blühende, die Unentdeckte,
in der es hundert Wege gibt.

Da liessen sie sie gehn und schweben
und treiben mit dem jungen Jahr;
ihr dienendes Marien-Leben
ward königlich und wunderbar.
Wie feiertägliches Geläute
ging es durch alle Häuser gross;
und die einst mädchenhaft Zerstreute
war so versenkt in ihren Schoss
und so erfüllt von jenem Einen
und so für Tausende genug,
dass alles schien, sie zu bescheinen,
die wie ein Weinberg war und trug.

12

And then that girl the angels came to visit,
she woke also to fruit, frightened by beauty,
given love, shy, in her
so much blossom, the forest
no one had explored, with paths leading everywhere.

They left her alone to walk and to drift
and the spring carried her along.
Her simple and unselfcentered Mary-life
became marvelous and castlelike.
Her life resembled trumpets on the feast days
that reverberated far inside every house;
and she, once so girlish and fragmented,
was so plunged now inside her womb,
and so full inside from that one thing
and so full—enough for a thousand others—
that every creature seemed to throw light on her
and she was like a slope with vines, heavily bearing.

Ich kann nicht glauben, dass der kleine Tod,
dem wir doch täglich übern Scheitel schauen,
uns eine Sorge bleibt und eine Not.

Ich kann nicht glauben, dass er ernsthaft droht;
ich lebe noch, ich habe Zeit zu bauen:
mein Blut ist länger als die Rosen rot.

Mein Sinn ist tiefer als das witzige Spiel
mit unsrer Furcht, darin er sich gefällt.
Ich bin die Welt,
aus der er irrend fiel.

                        Wie er
kreisende Mönche wandern so umher;
man fürchtet sich vor ihrer Wiederkehr,
man weiss nicht: ist es jedesmal derselbe,
sinds zwei, sinds zehn, sinds tausend oder mehr?
Man kennt nur diese fremde gelbe Hand,
die sich ausstreckt so nackt und nah—
da, da:
als käm sie aus dem eigenen Gewand.

13

I can hardly believe that this tiny death,
over whose head we look every day we wake,
is still such a threat to us and so much trouble.

I really can't take his growls seriously.
I am still in my body, I have time to build,
my blood will be red long after the rose is gone.

My grasp of things is deeper than the clever games
he finds it fun to play with our fears.
I am the solid world
from which he slipped and fell.

                              He is like
those monks in cloisters that walk around and around;
one feels a fear when they approach:
one doesn't know—is it the same one every time,
are there two, are there ten, a thousand monks, more?
All one knows is the strange yellow hand,
which is reaching out so naked and so close . . .
there it is,
as if it came out of your own clothes.

So ist mein Tagwerk, über dem
mein Schatten liegt wie eine Schale.
Und bin ich auch wie Laub und Lehm,
sooft ich bete oder male,
ist Sonntag, und ich bin im Tale
ein jubelndes Jerusalem.

Ich bin die stolze Stadt des Herrn
und sage ihn mit hundert Zungen;
in mir ist Davids Dank verklungen:
ich lag in Harfendämmerungen
und atmete den Abendstern.

Nach Aufgang gehen meine Gassen.
Und bin ich lang vom Volk verlassen,
so ists: damit ich grösser bin.
Ich höre jeden in mir schreiten
und breite meine Einsamkeiten
von Anbeginn zu Anbeginn.

14

This is my labor—over it
my shadow lies like the shell of a nut.
It's true I'm the same as leaves and mud,
but as often as I pray or paint
it is Sunday, and in the valley I am
a jubilant Jerusalem.

I am the proud city of the Lord,
and praise him with a hundred tongues;
David's thanks have found a resonance in me;
I lay in the twilight of harps
and breathed in the evening star.

My streets rise toward sunrise.
After people have left me alone a long time
it happens that I am larger.
Inside me I hear steps ring
and I stretch my loneliness out
from eternity to eternity.

Ihr vielen unbestürmten Städte,
habt ihr euch nie den Feind ersehnt?
O dass er euch belagert hätte
ein langes schwankendes Jahrzehnt.

Bis ihr ihn trostlos und in Trauern,
bis dass ihr hungernd ihn ertrugt;
er liegt wie Landschaft vor den Mauern,
denn also weiss er auszudauern
um jene, die er heimgesucht.

Schaut aus vom Rande eurer Dächer:
da lagert er und wird nicht matt
und wird nicht weniger und schwächer
und schickt nicht Droher und Versprecher
und Überreder in die Stadt.

Er ist der grosse Mauerbrecher,
der eine stumme Arbeit hat.

15

All of you undisturbed cities,
haven't you ever longed for the Enemy?
I'd like to see you besieged by him
for ten endless and ground-shaking years.

Until you were desperate and mad with suffering;
finally in hunger you would feel his weight.
He lies outside the walls like a countryside.
And he knows very well how to endure
longer than the ones he comes to visit.

Climb up on your roofs and look out:
his camp is there, and his morale doesn't falter,
and his numbers do not decrease; he will not grow weaker,
and he sends no one into the city to threaten
or promise, and no one to negotiate.

He is the one who breaks down the walls,
and when he works, he works in silence.

Es tauchten tausend Theologen
in deines Namens alte Nacht.
Jungfrauen sind zu dir erwacht,
und Jünglinge in Silber zogen
und schimmerten in dir, du Schlacht.

In deinen langen Bogengängen
begegneten die Dichter sich
und waren Könige von Klängen
und mild und tief und meisterlich.

Du bist die sanfte Abendstunde,
die alle Dichter ähnlich macht;
du drängst dich dunkel in die Munde,
und im Gefühl von einem Fund
umgibt ein jeder dich mit Pracht.

Dich heben hunderttausend Harfen
wie Schwingen aus der Schweigsamkeit.
Und deine alten Winde warfen
zu allen Dingen und Bedarfen
den Hauch von deiner Herrlichkeit.

16

How many thousands of divinity students
have dipped their bodies into the old night of your name.
What the girls waken to is you,
and when the young men dressed in silver weave
and flash in battle—that is also you.

The poets always met
in your long vaulted corridors.
And they were emperors of pure sound
and moving and deep and assured.

You are the delicate hour at nightfall
that makes all the poets equally good;
you crowd full of darkness into their mouths,
and every poet, sensing he has discovered greatness,
surrounds you with magnificent things.

A hundred thousand harps take you
like wings and sweep you up out of silence.
And your primitive wind is blowing
the fragrance of your marvelous power
to every being and to every creature in need.

Wie der Wächter in den Weingeländen
seine Hütte hat und wacht,
bin ich Hütte, Herr, in deinen Händen
und bin Nacht, o Herr, von deiner Nacht.

Weinberg, Weide, alter Apfelgarten,
Acker, der kein Frühjahr überschlägt,
Feigenbaum, der auch im marmorharten
Grunde hundert Früchte trägt:

Duft geht aus aus deinen runden Zweigen.
Und du fragst nicht, ob ich wachsam sei;
furchtlos, aufgelöst in Säften, steigen
deine Tiefen still an mir vorbei.

17

Just as the watchman in the wine fields
has a shed for himself and keeps awake,
I am the shed in your arms, Lord,
my night is drawn from your night.

Vineyard, meadow, weathered apple orchard,
field that never lets a spring go by,
fig tree rooted in ground hard
as marble, yet carrying a hundred figs:

odor pours out from your heavy boughs,
and you never ask if I am keeping watch or not;
confident, dissolved by the juices, your depths
keep climbing past me silently.

In diesem Dorfe steht das letzte Haus
so einsam wie das letzte Haus der Welt.

Die Strasse, die das kleine Dorf nicht hält,
geht langsam weiter in die Nacht hinaus.

Das kleine Dorf ist nur ein Übergang
zwischen zwei Weiten, ahnungsvoll und bang,
ein Weg an Häusern hin statt eines Stegs.

Und die das Dorf verlassen, wandern lang,
und viele sterben vielleicht unterwegs.

18

In this town the last house stands
as lonely as if it were the last house in the world.

The highway, which the tiny town is not able to stop,
slowly goes deeper out into the night.

The tiny town is only a passing-over place,
worried and afraid, between two huge spaces—
a path running past houses instead of a bridge.

And those who leave the town wander a long way off
and many perhaps die on the road.

Manchmal steht einer auf beim Abendbrot
und geht hinaus und geht und geht und geht,—
weil eine Kirche wo im Osten steht.

Und seine Kinder segnen ihn wie tot.

Und einer, welcher stirbt in seinem Haus,
bleibt drinnen wohnen, bleibt in Tisch und Glas,
so dass die Kinder in die Welt hinaus
zu jener Kirche ziehn, die er vergass.

19

Sometimes a man stands up during supper
and walks outdoors, and keeps on walking,
because of a church that stands somewhere in the East.

And his children say blessings on him as if he were dead.

And another man, who remains inside his own house,
stays there, inside the dishes and in the glasses,
so that his children have to go far out into the world
toward that same church, which he forgot.

Die Könige der Welt sind alt
und werden keine Erben haben.
Die Söhne sterben schon als Knaben,
und ihre bleichen Töchter gaben
die Kranken Kronen der Gewalt.

Der Pöbel bricht sie klein zu Gelld,
der zeitgemässe Herr der Welt
dehnt sie im Feuer zu Maschinen,
die seinem Wollen grollend dienen;
aber das Glück ist nicht mit ihnen.

Das Erz hat Heimweh. Und verlassen
will es die Münzen und die Räder,
die es ein kleines Leben lehren.
Und aus Fabriken und aus Kassen
wird es zurück in das Geäder
der aufgetanen Berge kehren,
die sich verschliessen hinter ihm.

20

The kings of the world are growing old,
and they shall have no inheritors.
Their sons died while they were boys,
and their neurasthenic daughters abandoned
the sick crown to the mob.

The mob breaks it into tiny bits of gold.
The Lord of the World, master of the age,
melts them in fire into machines,
which do his orders with low growls;
but luck is not on their side.

The ore feels homesick. It wants to abandon
the minting houses and the wheels
that offer it such a meager life.
And out of factories and payroll boxes
it wants to go back into the veins
of the thrown-open mountain,
which will close again behind it.

Jetzt reifen schon die roten Berberitzen,
alternde Astern atmen schwach im Beet.
Wer jetzt nicht reich ist, da der Sommer geht,
wird immer warten und sich nie besitzen.

Wer jetzt nicht seine Augen schliessen kann,
gewiss, dass eine Fülle von Gesichten
in ihm nur wartet bis die Nacht begann,
um sich in seinem Dunkel aufzurichten:—
der ist vergangen wie ein alter Mann.

Dem kommt nichts mehr, dem stösst kein Tag mehr zu,
und alles lügt ihn an, was ihm geschieht;
auch du, mein Gott. Und wie ein Stein bist du,
welcher ihn täglich in die Tiefe zieht.

21

Already the ripening barberries are red,
and the old asters hardly breathe in their beds.
The man who is not rich now as summer goes
will wait and wait and never be himself.

The man who cannot quietly close his eyes,
certain that there is vision after vision
inside, simply waiting until nighttime
to rise all around him in the darkness—
it's all over for him, he's like an old man.

Nothing else will come; no more days will open,
and everything that does happen will cheat him.
Even you, my God. And you are like a stone
that draws him daily deeper into the depths.

Vielleicht, dass ich durch schwere Berge gehe
in harten Adern, wie ein Erz allein;
und bin so tief, dass ich kein Ende sehe
und keine Ferne: alles wurde Nähe
und alle Nähe wurde Stein.

Ich bin ja noch kein Wissender im Wehe,—
so macht mich dieses grosse Dunkel klein;
bist *Du* es aber: mach dich schwer, brich ein:
dass deine ganze Hand an mir geschehe
und ich an dir mit meinem ganzen Schrein.

22

It's possible I am pushing through solid rock
in flintlike layers, as the ore lies, alone;
I am such a long way in I see no way through,
and no space: everything is close to my face,
and everything close to my face is stone.

I don't have much knowledge yet in grief—
so this massive darkness makes me small.
You be the master: make yourself fierce, break in:
then your great transforming will happen to me,
and my great grief cry will happen to you.

Denn, Herr, die grossen Städte sind
verlorene und aufgelöste;
wie Flucht vor Flammen ist die grösste,—
und ist kein Trost, dass er sie tröste,
und ihre kleine Zeit verrinnt.

Da leben Menschen, leben schlecht und schwer,
in tiefen Zimmern, bange von Gebärde,
geängsteter denn eine Erstlingsherde;
und draussen wacht und atmet deine Erde,
sie aber sind und wissen es nicht mehr.

Da wachsen Kinder auf an Fensterstufen,
die immer in demselben Schatten sind,
und wissen nicht, dass draussen Blumen rufen
zu einem Tag voll Weite, Glück und Wind,—
und müssen Kind sein und sind traurig Kind.

Da blühen Jungfraun auf zum Unbekannten
und sehnen sich nach ihrer Kindheit Ruh;
das aber ist nicht da, wofür sie brannten,
und zitternd schliessen sie sich wieder zu.
Und haben in verhüllten Hinterzimmern
die Tage der enttäuschten Mutterschaft,
der langen Nächte willenloses Wimmern
und kalte Jahre ohne Kampf und Kraft.
Und ganz im Dunkel stehn die Sterbebetten,
und langsam sehnen sie sich dazu hin;
und sterben lange, sterben wie in Ketten
und gehen aus wie eine Bettlerin.

23

And the great cities, Lord, what are they?
Places disintegrating and abandoned.
The city I know resembles animals fleeing from a fire.
The shelter it gave has no shelter now,
and the age of the cities is nearly over.

Men and women live there, stunned, thinned out,
in darkened rooms, afraid of any human gesture,
more fearful than a herd of yearling steers.
Your earth opens its eyes and breathes,
but they are no longer aware of the breathing.

A child lives its growing years at a windowsill.
The shadow makes the same angle there each day.
It doesn't realize that there are wild roses calling
to a day of open places, gaiety and wind.
It has to be a child and becomes a sad child.

And young women blossom upward toward the unknown
and feel a longing for the peace of childhood;
what they are burning for, however, is not in the world
and their body trembles as they close themselves once more.
And the disappointed years of being a mother
go by in apartments out of the light.
Night after night they have no will and weep,
cold years go by with no power and no real battle.
The deathbed waits in a still darker room,
and they wish themselves slowly slowly into it,
and they take a long time to die, as if in chains,
and die still dependent on others, as beggars are.

O wo ist er, der Klare, hingeklungen?
Was fühlen ihn, den Jubelnden und Jungen,
die Armen, welche harren, nicht von fern?

Was steigt er nicht in ihre Dämmerungen—
 der Armut grosser Abendstern.

24

And where is he, the clear one, whose tone rings to us?
Why don't the poor feel him, the rejoicing one,
mastering us, the young one, even though far off?

Why doesn't he climb then in their dusk—
    the great evening star of poverty.

FROM The Book of Pictures

(*Das Buch der Bilder*)

1902–1906

CLARA WESTHOFF had been a student of Rodin. Through her, Rilke received a commission to write a monograph on the sculptor. He was twenty-six when he arrived in Paris. With that move, he became a European, and a city poet as well, living on the edge of poverty. *The Notebooks of Malte Laurids Brigge* contains some of this Paris life. Rilke's superb gift for the image helped him to grasp what he saw there and to understand why it frightened him. He discovered that faces wear out. In the old days, faces were made to last a whole lifetime, but now sometimes the face grows thin, and the "no-face" begins to show through. He found himself thinking that after the industrial revolution the ready-made death dominates—the stroke death, the heart-attack death, the accident death, the cancer death. . . . They were all ready-made, and one simply stepped into one or the other as into ready-made clothes. "O Lord, give each person his own personal death."

Rilke had begun a way of living that later—except for visits to castles or the apartments of the rich—became typical for him: a city, not much money, one respectable suit, a small room, often on a noisy street because it takes money to purchase silence, meals eaten alone in a dairy restaurant, a sense of being hunted, living as an outsider, the richness all hidden in his chest, none visible on the outside. He would rent a room, and next door a man would play the violin till late at night. This had happened in so many cities.

> *Strange violin, are you following me?*
> *In how many distant cities already*
> *has your lonely night spoken to mine?*
> *Are a hundred playing you? Or only one? . . .*
>
> *Why am I always the neighbor to those men*
> *who force you in fear to sing*
> *and to say: The heaviness of life*
> *is heavier even than the weight of things.*

Rilke now began to notice the heaviness inside things—how much angry, even malevolent, energy there is in a blind man's cane, how much contagious despair in the chair inherited with a furnished room, especially in the shiny spot on the chair back where so many failed introverts have leaned their heads. He feels utterly out of place in a middle-class living room. Sofas are so packed with gross energy they terrify the unconscious.

His poem "The Solitary Person" helped me so much in my twenties. Like many others of my generation, I was trying to live for my talent or maybe for "the infinite," with almost no money, in a rented room with one chair and a table, not talking. What a shock it was to go home for Thanksgiving. The sofas and the self-confident turkey said that the life I was leading was wrong; they were right. But Rilke's poems say to the young man or woman that the "objectless" life they are leading is not wrong. The not fitting in they experience comes from the best part of themselves, not the weakest part, and the pain is the cracking of the walls as the room grows. Writing these poems, Rilke is not an aesthete, but a wise grandfather.

During his first four years in Paris he worked on an intense book called *Das Buch der Bilder,* the mood very different from the mood of his first book. The title translates as a book of images or paintings. I've called it *The Book of Pictures* to emphasize that he is not writing a literary book about images but rather a painterly book in which he adopts some of the disciplines of painting.

"From Childhood" is an example. This poem, which describes how caught up he was in his mother as a boy, he composed the way a painter like Rembrandt composed a canvas. Rilke paints both background and foreground, the shadows and the light. Two figures only are painted in, the boy and his mother.

> *The darkness in the room was like enormous riches;*
> *there the child was sitting, wonderfully alone.*
> *And when the mother entered, as if in a dream,*
> *a glass quaked in the silent china closet.*
> *She felt it, how the room was betraying her,*
> *and kissed her child, saying, "Are you here?"*
> *Then both looked toward the piano in fear,*

for often at evening she would have a song
in which the child found himself strangely caught.

Among the furniture, a single glass is lit up and the large dark piano. As a painter must, he chooses one instant to stand for the whole flowing relationship: the moment the mother plays the song. The mother's hand with its big ring moves eternally over the keys, and the boy eternally watches.

He sat alone still. His great gaze hung
upon her hand, which, totally bowed down by the ring,
walked over the white keys
as if plowing through deep drifts of snow.

I once heard a story of Rilke's early life with his mother. It seems she wanted a girl, not a boy; and she gave him seven or eight middle names, including Maria. When he was two or three years old, Rilke would knock on the living room door from the hall. "Who is it . . . is it Rainer?" "No, that naughty Rainer is dead." "Is it Margaret?" "Yes." "Well, then you can come in." Rilke would then enter, wearing a small dress, and he and his mother would have tea. I tell this story because so often his critics omit, in the interest of aesthetics, the root details of his life. American critics tend to write of Rilke's using an elaborate and attenuated language, praising so justly his powers of discrimination, that we don't realize what a fierce and sordid struggle he fought with his mother—like Kafka with his father. He fought through and won. Without cunning, courage, and discipline, Rilke would have been wiped out.

The mood of *The Book of Pictures* is psychic change, the mood when the soul ground is shaken. There are times for all of us when the poles of life become inexplicably reversed, the feelings go naked, one is exposed; and yet one is pleased that some old dependencies, especially a shameful dependence on comfort, are ending. Robert Lowell mentions it at the end of "The Exile's Return": "and your life is in your hands." Rilke opens his picture book with the poem "Entrance" or "The Way In," in which the young, doubtful, world-shy, room-loving writer is urged to leave what he knows so well.

Whoever you are: some evening take a step
out of your house, which you know so well.
Enormous space is near, your house lies where it begins,
whoever you are.
Your eyes find it hard to tear themselves
from the sloping threshold, but with your eyes
slowly, slowly, lift one black tree
up, so it stands against the sky: skinny, alone.
With that you have made the World. The world is immense
and like a word that is still growing in the silence.
In the same moment that your will grasps it,
your eyes, feeling its subtlety, will leave it. . . .

In the masterpiece "The Man Watching," Rilke pours out his
substance in generous rivers.

I can tell by the way the trees beat, after
so many dull days, on my worried windowpanes
that a storm is coming,
and I hear the far-off fields say things
I can't bear without a friend,
I can't love without a sister.

The storm, the shifter of shapes, drives on
across the woods and across time,
and the world looks as if it had no age:
the landscape, like a line in the psalm book,
is seriousness and weight and eternity.

What we choose to fight is so tiny!
What fights with us is so great!

Rilke then moves to shape and contain the picture of fighting
by means better known to painters than to poets. A poet might
list many examples of struggle—with a dragon, with a teacher,
with a woman, because language can move through time. Rilke
chooses one pair of fighters, Jacob and the Angel, and says every-
thing through them. He has chosen as if he were a sculptor,
and he treats the two figures as if he were sculpting bodies:

I mean the Angel who appeared
to the wrestlers of the Old Testament:
when the wrestler's sinews

grew long like metal strings,
he felt them under his fingers
like chords of deep music.

So the discipline of concentration here is a gift from painters and sculptors. The waters that flowed through his first book have become stronger. Leaving behind the triumphant joy of longing, Rilke stands alone with his own life, not triumphant, not defeated, watching a sunset.

Slowly the west reaches for clothes of new colors
which it passes to a row of ancient trees.
You look, and soon these two worlds both leave you,
one part climbs towards heaven, one sinks to earth . . .

leaving you (it is impossible to untangle the threads)
your own life, timid and standing high and growing,
so that, sometimes blocked in, sometimes reaching out,
one moment your life is a stone in you, and the next, a star.

By now he has learned to write not only out of the assurance that his underground water is inexhaustible, but also out of the quivering of growth, so close to defeat, when the whole life seems in doubt; perhaps it is a life lived by a fool. He values that sensation of failure. He eats the shock for the sake of the seed. And he writes more fall poems. He feels a truth in fall expressed by the sound of dry leaves scraping along a street.

Whoever has no house by now will not build.
Whoever is alone now will remain alone,
will wait up, read, write long letters,
and walk along sidewalks under large trees,
not going home, as the leaves fall and blow away.

He holds the reader to a sense of how alone the soul is.

We're all falling. This hand here is falling.
And look at the other one. . . . It's in them all.

Rilke wanted to provide readers with a book that would be like a big room full of paintings. Here the man or woman who resists the collective can enter and walk around; no one will bother him or demand conversation. The stroller can go up to one of the poems in the book and look at it closely, for its detail, and then back away and look from a distance. Rilke avoids the old moral poem with its closing couplet; when his poem ends it is still moving. He simply passes the poem to the reader, and goes back to his solitude. Vermeer often paints an open window, perhaps to suggest outer space; a room's interior to suggest inner space; a map on the wall to suggest roads; and, finally, a mysterious shape seen from the back. Rilke's poems are surprisingly intimate, and yet he has a reserve like Akhmatova's: he tells and he doesn't tell. In a poem like "Moving Forward" there is no evasive persona as in Eliot's work; we see Rilke looking at a painting. When he is growing, he says, he feels that dogs and trees are relatives, and that he can see farther into a painting, see into it more deeply.

> *The deep parts of my life pour onward,*
> *as if the river shores were opening out.*
> *It seems that things are more like me now,*
> *that I can see farther into paintings.*
> *I feel closer to what language can't reach.*
> *With my senses, as with birds, I climb*
> *into the windy heaven, out of the oak,*
> *and in the ponds broken off from the sky*
> *my feeling sinks, as if standing on fishes.*

The last two lines in German are:

> *und in den abgebrochnen Tag der Teiche*
> *sinkt, wie auf Fischen stehend, mein Gefühl.*

I have always loved these lines, the fish image is a triumph, an amazing union of senses. It embodies exultation, humility, and danger in a single image. And we feel that the image doesn't say less than the truth, nor more than the truth. A translator can sometimes carry over such an image if it is vivid; but Rilke's elaborate and thoroughgoing labor on sound cannot be conveyed. In English his poems sound colorless. I've tried for ten years to get the last three lines of "October Day" right, with their lonely sound of blowing leaves and their pride in solitude, but I can't do it. So the reader shouldn't believe he has the power here of the poems in German.

68

The first edition of *Das Buch der Bilder* was published in 1902. Rilke added a few poems for the second edition, among them the ten called *The Voices*, which I've included in this collection. Rilke sent them to his publisher with a note, in which he remarks that perhaps this group will "keep the book from being purely aesthetic." I think he means that his sensibility is not the point of these poems. Translating them, one has to try to catch the voice tone of suicides, and the thought rhythms of mad people. The poems are a leap across the gap between people. To play his part, the reader should read them aloud.

Eingang

Wer du auch seist: Am Abend tritt hinaus
aus deiner Stube, drin du alles weisst;
als letztes vor der Ferne liegt dein Haus:
Wer du auch seist.
Mit deinen Augen, welche müde kaum
von der verbrauchten Schwelle sich befrein,
hebst du ganz langsam einen schwarzen Baum
und stellst ihn vor den Himmel: schlank, allein.
Und hast die Welt gemacht. Und sie ist gross
und wie ein Wort, das noch im Schweigen reift.
Und wie dein Wille ihren Sinn begreift,
lassen sie deine Augen zärtlich los . . .

The Way In

Whoever you are: some evening take a step
out of your house, which you know so well.
Enormous space is near, your house lies where it begins,
whoever you are.
Your eyes find it hard to tear themselves
from the sloping threshold, but with your eyes
slowly, slowly, lift one black tree
up, so it stands against the sky: skinny, alone.
With that you have made the world. The world is immense
and like a word that is still growing in the silence.
In the same moment that your will grasps it,
your eyes, feeling its subtlety, will leave it. . . .

Kindheit

Da rinnt der Schule lange Angst und Zeit
mit Warten hin, mit lauter dumpfen Dingen.
O Einsamkeit, o schweres Zeitverbringen . . .
Und dann hinaus: die Strassen sprühn und klingen,
und auf den Plätzen die Fontänen springen,
und in den Gärten wird die Welt so weit.—
Und durch das alles gehn im kleinen Kleid,
ganz anders als die andern gehn und gingen—:
O wunderliche Zeit, o Zeitverbringen,
o Einsamkeit.

Und in das alles fern hinauszuschauen:
Männer und Frauen; Männer, Männer, Frauen
und Kinder, welche anders sind und bunt;
und da ein Haus und dann und wann ein Hund
und Schrecken lautlos wechselnd mit Vertrauen—:
O Trauer ohne Sinn, o Traum, o Grauen,
o Tiefe ohne Grund.

Und so zu spielen: Ball und Ring und Reifen
in einem Garten, welcher sanft verblasst,
und manchmal die Erwachsenen zu streifen
blind und verwildert in des Haschens Hast,
aber am Abend still, mit kleinen steifen
Schritten nach Haus zu gehn, fest angefasst—:
O immer mehr entweichendes Begreifen,
o Angst, o Last.

Und stundenlang am grossen grauen Teiche
mit einem kleinen Segelschiff zu knien;
es zu vergessen, weil noch andre, gleiche
und schönere Segel durch die Ringe ziehn,

Childhood

Time in school drags along with so much worry,
and waiting, things so dumb and stupid.
Oh loneliness, oh heavy lumpish time . . .
Free at last: lights and colors and noises;
water leaps out of fountains into the air,
and the world is so huge in the woody places.
And moving through it in your short clothes,
and you don't walk the way the others do—
Such marvelous time, such time passing on,
such loneliness.

How strange to see into it all from far away:
men and women, there's a man, one more woman;
children's bright colors make them stand out;
and here a house and now and then a dog
and terror all at once replaced by total trust—
What crazy mourning, what dream, what heaviness,
what deepness without end.

And playing: a hoop, and a bat, and a ball,
in some green place as the light fades away.
And not noticing, you brush against a grownup,
rushing blindly around in tag, half-crazed,
but when the light fades you go with small
puppety steps home, your hand firmly held—
Such oceanic vision that is fading,
such a constant worry, such weight.

Sometimes also kneeling for hours on end
with a tiny sailboat at a grayish pond,
all forgotten because sails more beautiful
than yours go on crossing the circles;

und denken müssen an das kleine bleiche
Gesicht, das sinkend aus dem Teiche schien—:
O Kindheit, o entgleitende Vergleiche,
wohin? Wohin?

and one had to think always about the pale
narrow face looking up as it sank down—
Oh childhood, what was us going away,
going where? Where?

Aus einer Kindheit

Das Dunkeln war wie Reichtum in dem Raume,
darin der Knabe, sehr verheimlicht, sass.
Und als die Mutter eintrat wie im Traume,
erzitterte im stillen Schrank ein Glas.
Sie fühlte, wie das Zimmer sie verriet,
und küsste ihren Knaben; Bist du hier? . . .
Dann schauten beide bang nach dem Klavier,
denn manchen Abend hatte sie ein Lied,
darin das Kind sich seltsam tief verfing.

Er sass sehr still. Sein grosses Schauen hing
an ihrer Hand, die ganz gebeugt vom Ringe,
als ob sie schwer in Schneewehn ginge,
über die weissen Tasten ging.

From Childhood

The darkness in the room was like enormous riches;
there the child was sitting, wonderfully alone.
And when the mother entered, as if in a dream,
a glass quaked in the silent china closet.
She felt it, how the room was betraying her,
and kissed her child, saying, "Are you here?"
Then both looked toward the piano in fear,
for often at evening they would have a song
in which the child found himself strangely caught.

He sat stone still. His great gaze hung
upon her hand, which, totally bowed down by the ring,
walked over the white keys
as if plowing through deep drifts of snow.

Vorgefühl

Ich bin wie eine Fahne von Fernen umgeben.
Ich ahne die Winde, die kommen, und muss sie leben,
während die Dinge unten sich noch nicht rühren:
Die Türen schliessen noch sanft, und in den Kaminen ist Stille;
die Fenster zittern noch nicht, und der Staub ist noch schwer.

Da weiss ich die Stürme schon und bin erregt wie das Meer.
Und breite mich aus und falle in mich hinein
und werfe mich ab und bin ganz allein
in dem grossen Sturm.

Sense of Something Coming

I am like a flag in the center of open space.
I sense ahead the wind which is coming, and must live
it through,
while the things of the world still do not move:
the doors still close softly, and the chimneys are full
of silence,
the windows do not rattle yet, and the dust still lies down.

I already know the storm, and I am as troubled as the sea.
I leap out, and fall back,
and throw myself out, and am absolutely alone
in the great storm.

Einsamkeit

Die Einsamkeit ist wie ein Regen.
Sie steigt vom Meer den Abenden entgegen;
von Ebenen, die fern sind und entlegen,
geht sie zum Himmel, der sie immer hat.
Und erst vom Himmel fällt sie auf die Stadt.

Regnet hernieder in den Zwitterstunden,
wenn sich nach Morgen wenden alle Gassen
und wenn die Leiber, welche nichts gefunden,
enttäuscht und traurig voneinander lassen;
und wenn die Menschen, die einander hassen,
in einem Bett zusammen schlafen müssen:

dann geht die Einsamkeit mit den Flüssen . . .

Loneliness

Being apart and lonely is like rain.
It climbs toward evening from the ocean plains;
from flat places, rolling and remote, it climbs
to heaven, which is its old abode.
And only when leaving heaven drops upon the city.

It rains down on us in those twittering
hours when the streets turn their face to the dawn,
and when two bodies who have found nothing,
disappointed and depressed, roll over;
and when two people who despise each other
have to sleep together in one bed—

that is when loneliness receives the rivers. . . .

Menschen bei Nacht

Die Nächte sind nicht für die Menge gemacht.
Von deinem Nachbar trennt dich die Nacht,
und du sollst ihn nicht suchen trotzdem.
Und machst du nachts deine Stube licht,
um Menschen zu schauen ins Angesicht,
so musst du bedenken: wem.

Die Menschen sind furchtbar vom Licht entstellt,
das von ihren Gesichtern träuft,
und haben sie nachts sich zusammengesellt,
so schaust du eine wankende Welt
durcheinandergehäuft.
Auf ihren Stirnen hat gelber Schein
alle Gedanken verdrängt,
in ihren Blicken flackert der Wein,
an ihren Händen hängt
die schwere Gebärde, mit der sie sich
bei ihren Gesprächen verstehn;
und dabei sagen sie: *Ich* und *Ich*
und meinen: Irgendwen.

Human Beings at Night

Nights are not made for the masses.
Night separates you from your neighbor,
and you're not to go find him and defy that.
And if you do light your room at night
so that you can see the faces of people,
you have to think: who is it?

People are horribly disfigured by light,
which falls in drops from their faces.
And if they've all gotten together one night,
you're looking at a very shaky world
all thrown together any which way.
The yellow lamp has driven every
thought out of their heads,
wine flickers in their eyes,
and from their hands those heavy
gestures are hanging with which they
make themselves understood in their conversations—
and with those gestures they say "I" and "I"
and mean "Anybody."

Abend

Der Abend wechselt langsam die Gewänder,
die ihm ein Rand von alten Bäumen halt;
du schaust: und von dir scheiden sich die Länder,
ein himmelfahrendes und eins, das fällt;

und lassen dich, zu keinem ganz gehörend,
nicht ganz so dunkel wie das Haus, das schweigt,
hicht ganz so sicher Ewiges beschwörend
wie das, was Stern wird jede Nacht und steigt—

und lassen dir (unsäglich zu entwirrn)
dein Leben bang und riesenhaft und reifend,
so dass es, bald begrenzt und begreifend,
abwechselnd Stein in dir wird und Gestirn.

Sunset

Slowly the west reaches for clothes of new colors
which it passes to a row of ancient trees.
You look, and soon these two worlds both leave you,
one part climbs toward heaven, one sinks to earth,

leaving you, not really belonging to either,
not so hopelessly dark as that house that is silent,
not so unswervingly given to the eternal as that thing
that turns to a star each night and climbs—

leaving you (it is impossible to untangle the threads)
your own life, timid and standing high and growing,
so that, sometimes blocked in, sometimes reaching out,
one moment your life is a stone in you, and the next, a star.

Der Einsame

Wie einer, der auf fremden Meeren fuhr,
so bin ich bei den ewig Einheimischen;
die vollen Tage stehn auf ihren Tischen,
mir aber ist die Ferne voll Figur.

In mein Gesicht reicht eine Welt herein,
die vielleicht unbewohnt ist wie ein Mond,
sie aber lassen kein Gefühl allein,
und alle ihre Worte sind bewohnt.

Die Dinge, die ich weither mit mir nahm,
sehn selten aus, gehalten an das Ihre—:
in ihrer grossen Heimat sind sie Tiere,
hier halten sie den Atem an vor Scham.

The Solitary Person

Among so many people cozy in their homes,
I am like a man who explores far-off oceans.
Days with full stomachs stand on their tables;
I see a distant land full of images.

I sense another world close to me,
perhaps no more lived in than the moon;
they, however, never let a feeling alone,
and all the words they use are so worn.

The living things I brought back with me
hardly peep out, compared with all they own.
In their native country they were wild;
here they hold their breath from shame.

Herbst

Die Blätter fallen, fallen wie von weit,
als welkten in den Himmeln ferne Gärten;
sie fallen mit verneinender Gebärde.

Und in den Nächten fällt die schwere Erde
aus allen Sternen in die Einsamkeit.

Wir alle fallen. Diese Hand da fällt.
Und sieh dir andre an: es ist in allen.

Und doch ist Einer, welcher dieses Fallen
unendlich sanft in seinen Händen hält.

Autumn

The leaves are falling, falling as if from far up,
as if orchards were dying high in space.
Each leaf falls as if it were motioning "no."

And tonight the heavy earth is falling
away from all the other stars in the loneliness.

We're all falling. This hand here is falling.
And look at the other one. . . . It's in them all.

And yet there is Someone, whose hands
infinitely calm, hold up all this falling.

Sturm

Wenn die Wolken, von Stürmen geschlagen,
jagen:
Himmel von hundert Tagen
über einem einzigen Tag—:

Dann fühl ich dich, Hejtman, von fern
(der du deine Kosaken gern
zu dem grössten Herrn
führen wolltest).
Deinen wagrechten Nacken
fühl ich, Mazeppa.

Dann bin auch ich an das rasende Rennen
eines rauchenden Rückens gebunden;
alle Dinge sind mir verschwunden,
nur die Himmel kann ich erkennen:

Überdunkelt and überschienen
lieg ich flach unter ihnen,
wie Ebenen liegen;
meine Augen sind offen wie Teiche,
und in ihnen flüchtet das gleiche
Fliegen.

Storm

When the clouds driven by winds
go galloping by—
heavens of a hundred days
passing over a single day—

Then I feel close to you, Hetman
(you who tried to deliver
your cossacks
to the strongest of the barons).
I feel your neck bound horizontal to the earth,
Mazeppa.

Then I am also tied on the excited horse,
tied to a steaming saddle;
all the earthly things have disappeared,
I can only see the skies:

drowning in shadow, drowning in light,
like the prairies
I lie flat.
My eyes resemble ponds
and moving shapes
flow across them.

Der Nachbar

Fremde Geige, gehst du mir nach?
In wieviel fernen Städten schon sprach
deine einsame Nacht zu meiner?
Spielen dich hunderte? Spielt dich einer?

Gibt es in allen grossen Städten
solche, die sich ohne dich
schon in den Flüssen verloren hätten?
Und warum trifft es immer mich?

Warum bin ich immer der Nachbar derer,
die dich bange zwingen zu singen
und zu sagen: Das Leben ist schwerer
als die Schwere von allen Dingen.

The Neighbor

Strange violin, are you following me?
In how many distant cities already
has your lonely night spoken to mine?
Are a hundred playing you? Or only one?

Are there in all the giant cities
men like this, who without you
would already be gone into the rivers?
And why am I always the one who hears it?

Why am I always the neighbor to those men
who force you in fear to sing
and to say: The heaviness of life
is heavier even than the weight of things.

Pont du Carrousel

Der blinde Mann, der auf der Brücke steht,
grau wie ein Markstein namenloser Reiche,
er ist vielleicht das Ding, das immer gleiche,
um das von fern die Sternenstunde geht,
und der Gestirne stiller Mittelpunkt.
Denn alles um ihn irrt und rinnt und prunkt.

Er ist der unbewegliche Gerechte,
in viele wirre Wege hingestellt;
der dunkle Eingang in die Unterwelt
bei einem oberflächlichen Geschlechte.

Pont du Carrousel

That blind man, standing on the bridge, as gray
as some abandoned empire's boundary stone,
perhaps he is the one thing that never shifts,
around which the stars move in their hours,
and the motionless hub of the constellations.
For the city drifts and rushes and struts around him.

He is the just man, the immovable
set down here in many tangled streets;
the dark opening to the underworld
among a superficial generation.

Die Aschanti

(Jardin d'Acclimatation)

Keine Vision von fremden Ländern,
kein Gefühl von braunen Frauen, die
tanzen aus den fallenden Gewändern.

Keine wilde fremde Melodie.
Keine Lieder, die vom Blute stammten,
und kein Blut, das aus den Tiefen schrie.

Keine braunen Mädchen, die sich samten
breiteten in Tropenmüdigkeit;
keine Augen, die wie Waffen flammten,

und die Munde zum Gelächter breit.
Und ein wunderliches Sich-verstehn
mit der hellen Menschen Eitelkeit.

Und mir war so bange hinzusehen.

O wie sind die Tiere so viel treuer,
die in Gittern auf und nieder gehn,
ohne Eintract mit dem Treiben neuer
fremder Dinge, die sie nicht verstehn;
und sie brennen wie ein stilles Feuer
leise aus und sinken in sich ein,
teilnahmslos dem neuen Abenteuer
und mit ihrem grossen Blut allein.

The Ashantis

(*Jardin d'Acclimatation*)

No images of unvisited countries,
no feeling of brown women
dancing out of their falling clothes.

No wild and unheard-of melodies.
No tunes that rise from the blood,
no blood calling from the deep places.

No young women brown and velvety,
who settle there in tropical exhaustion;
no eyes that flash like spears,

instead mouths stretched for laughing.
And a bizarre compromise
with the egotism of the white man.

I felt so much grief watching that.

How much more faith the animals have
that walk up and down in their cages,
having nothing to do with the jumble of new
strange objects that they don't understand;
and they burn like a fire with little air,
they burn, and fall into themselves,
they take no part in this new strangeness,
and are alone with their huge blood.

Abend in Skåne

Der Park ist hoch. Und wie aus einem Haus
tret ich aus seiner Dämmerung heraus
in Ebene und Abend. In den Wind,
denselben Wind, den auch die Wolken fühlen,
die hellen Flüsse und die Flügelmühlen,
die langsam mahlend stehn am Himmelsrand.
Jetzt bin auch ich ein Ding in seiner Hand,
das kleinste unter diesen Himmeln.—Schau:

Ist das ein Himmel?:
Selig lichtes Blau,
in das sich immer reinere Wolken drängen,
und drunter alle Weiss in Übergängen,
und drüber jenes dünne grosse Grau,
warmwallend wie auf roter Untermalung,
und über allem diese stille Strahlung
sinkender Sonne.

Wunderlicher Bau,
in sich bewegt und von sich selbst gehalten,
Gestalten bildend, Riesenflügel, Falten
und Hochgebirge vor den ersten Sternen
und plötzlich, da: Ein Tor in solche Fernen,
wie sie vielleicht nur Vögel kennen . . .

Evening in Skåne

These trees are high. As if leaving a house,
I walk out from their dusky light outdoors
into the open plains and the evening. And the wind,
the same wind the clouds feel,
the bright waters and the wheeling mills
that stand on the edge of the sky, grinding slowly.
Now I am also a thing of the world in your hands,
the tiniest under this sky. Look:

is that a sky?
Light and holy blue,
into which continually purer clouds are entering,
under them shade after shade of white,
and over it this thin-spun and huge gray
glowing as if shining through a red undercoat,
and rising above all of it this silent blazing light
of the sinking sun.

What a wonderful building,
moving inside itself, held up by itself,
forming figures, giant wings, canyons,
and high mountains, before the first star
and suddenly, there: a door so far off that maybe
only birds have ever felt that kind of distance. . . .

Fortschritt

Und wieder rauscht mein tiefes Leben lauter,
als ob es jetzt in breitern Ufern ginge.
Immer verwandter werden mir die Dinge
und alle Bilder immer angeschauter.
Dem Namenlosen fühl ich mich vertrauter:
Mit meinen Sinnen, wie mit Vögeln, reiche
ich in die windigen Himmel aus der Eiche,
und in den abgebrochnen Tag der Teiche
sinkt, wie auf Fischen stehend, mein Gefühl.

Moving Forward

The deep parts of my life pour onward,
as if the river shores were opening out.
It seems that things are more like me now,
that I can see farther into paintings.
I feel closer to what language can't reach.
With my senses, as with birds, I climb
into the windy heaven, out of the oak,
and in the ponds broken off from the sky
my feeling sinks, as if standing on fishes.

Herbsttag

Herr: es ist Zeit. Der Sommer war sehr gross.
Leg deinen Schatten auf die Sonnenuhren,
und auf den Fluren lass Winde los.

Befiehl den letzten Früchten voll zu sein;
gib ihnen noch zwei südlichere Tage,
dränge sie zur Vollendung hin und jage
die letzte Süsse in den schweren Wein.

Wer jetzt kein Haus hat, baut sich keines mehr.
Wer jetzt allein ist, wird es lange bleiben,
wird wachen, lesen, lange Briefe schreiben
und wird in den Alleen hin und her
unruhig wandern, wenn die Blätter treiben.

October Day

Oh Lord, it's time, it's time. It was a great summer.
Lay your shadow now on the sundials,
and on the open fields let the winds go!

Give the tardy fruits the hint to fill;
give them two more Mediterranean days,
drive them on into their greatness, and press
the final sweetness into the heavy wine.

Whoever has no house by now will not build.
Whoever is alone now will remain alone,
will wait up, read, write long letters,
and walk along sidewalks under large trees,
not going home, as the leaves fall and blow away.

Der Schauende

Ich sehe den Bäumen die Stürme an,
die aus laugewordenen Tagen
an meine ängstlichen Fenster schlagen,
und höre die Fernen Dinge sagen,
die ich nicht ohne Freund ertragen,
nicht ohne Schwester lieben kann.

Da geht der Sturm, ein Umgestalter,
geht durch den Wald und durch die Zeit,
und alles ist wie ohne Alter:
Die Landschaft, wie en Vers im Psalter,
ist Ernst und Wucht und Ewigkeit.

Wie ist das klein, womit wir ringen,
was mit uns ringt, wie ist das gross;
liessen wir, ähnlicher den Dingen,
uns *so* vom grossen Sturm bezwingen,
wir würden weit und namenlos.

Was wir besiegen, ist das Kleine,
und der Erfolg selbst macht uns klein.
Das Ewige und Ungemeine
will nicht von uns gebogen sein.
Das ist der Engel, der den Ringern
des Alten Testaments erschien:
wenn seiner Widersacher Sehnen
im Kampfe sich metallen dehnen,
fühlt er sie unter seinen Fingern
wie Saiten tiefer Melodien.

Wen dieser Engel überwand,
welcher so oft auf Kampf verzichtet,
der geht gerecht und aufgerichtet

The Man Watching

I can tell by the way the trees beat, after
so many dull days, on my worried windowpanes
that a storm is coming,
and I hear the far-off fields say things
I can't bear without a friend,
I can't love without a sister.

The storm, the shifter of shapes, drives on
across the woods and across time,
and the world looks as if it had no age:
the landscape, like a line in the psalm book,
is seriousness and weight and eternity.

What we choose to fight is so tiny!
What fights with us is so great!
If only we would let ourselves be dominated
as things do by some immense storm,
we would become strong too, and not need names.

When we win it's with small things,
and the triumph itself makes us small.
What is extraordinary and eternal
does not *want* to be bent by us.
I mean the Angel who appeared
to the wrestlers of the Old Testament:
when the wrestlers' sinews
grew long like metal strings,
he felt them under his fingers
like chords of deep music.

Whoever was beaten by this Angel
(who often simply declined the fight)
went away proud and strengthened

und gross aus jener harten Hand,
die sich, wie formend, ah ihn schmiegte,
Die Siege laden ihn nicht ein.
Sein Wachstum ist: Der Tiefbesiegte
von immer Grösserem zu sein.

and great from that harsh hand,
that kneaded him as if to change his shape.
Winning does not tempt that man.
This is how he grows: by being defeated, decisively,
by constantly greater beings.

The Voices

(Nine poems with a title poem)

Titelblatt

Die Reichen und Glücklichen haben gut schweigen,
niemand will wissen, was sie sind.
Aber die Dürftigen müssen sich zeigen,
müssen sagen: ich bin blind,
oder: ich bin im Begriff es zu werden
oder: es geht mir nicht gut auf Erden,
oder: ich habe ein krankes Kind,
oder: da bin ich zusammengefügt . . .

Und vielleicht, dass das gar nicht genügt.

Und weil alle sonst, wie an Dingen,
an ihnen vorbeigehn, müssen sie singen.

Und da hört man noch guten Gesang.

Freilich die Menschen sind seltsam; sie hören
lieber Kastraten in Knabenchören.

Aber Gott selber kommt und bleibt lang,
wenn ihn diese Beschnittenen stören.

Title Poem

It's O.K. for the rich and the lucky to keep still;
no one wants to know about them anyway.
But those in need have to step forward,
have to say: I am blind,
or: I'm about to go blind,
or: nothing is going well with me,
or: I have a child who is sick,
or: right there I'm sort of glued together. . . .

And probably that doesn't do anything either.

They have to sing; if they didn't sing, everyone
would walk past, as if they were fences or trees.

That's where you can hear good singing.

People really are strange: they prefer
to hear castratos in boy choirs.

But God himself comes and stays a long time
when the world of half-people start to bore him.

Das Lied des Bettlers

Ich gehe immer von Tor zu Tor,
verregnet und verbrannt;
auf einmal leg ich mein rechtes Ohr
in meine rechte Hand.
Dann kommt mir meine Stimme vor,
als hätt ich sie nie gekannt.

Dann weiss ich nicht sicher, wer da schreit,
ich oder irgendwer.
Ich schreie um eine Kleinigkeit.
Die Dichter schrein um mehr.

Und endlich mach ich noch mein Gesicht
mit beiden Augen zu;
wie's dann in der Hand liegt mit seinem Gewicht,
sieht es fast aus wie Ruh.
Damit sie nicht meinen, ich hätte nicht,
wohin ich mein Haupt tu.

The Song the Beggar Sings

I go all the time from door to door,
scorched, soaked to the skin.
Then all at once I lay my right ear down
in my right hand.
Then my voice seems strange to me,
and I've never heard it like that!

Then I don't know exactly who is calling,
me or someone else.
I cry out about a cent or two,
the poets cry about more.

Finally, using both my eyes
I close my face,
and when it lies with its weight in my hand
it looks almost like rest.
That's so they won't think I have nowhere
to lay my head.

Das Lied des Blinden

Ich bin blind, ihr draussen, das ist ein Fluch,
ein Widerwillen, ein Widerspruch,
etwas täglich Schweres.
Ich leg meine Hand auf den Arm der Frau,
meine graue Hand auf ihr graues Grau,
und sie führt mich durch lauter Leeres.

Ihr rührt euch und rückt und bildet euch ein,
anders zu klingen als Stein auf Stein,
aber ihr irrt euch: ich allein
lebe und leide und lärme.
In mir ist ein endloses Schrein,
und ich weiss nicht, schreit mir mein
Herz oder meine Gedärme.

Erkennt ihr die Lieder? Ihr sanget sie nicht,
nicht ganz in dieser Betonung.
Euch kommt jeden Morgen das neue Licht
warm in die offene Wohnung.
Und ihr habt ein Gefühl von Gesicht zu Gesicht,
und das verleitet zur Schonung.

The Song the Blind Man Sings

I am blind, you out there, that is a malediction,
an awful thing, a contradiction,
something heavy every day.
I lay my hand on the arm of the woman,
my gray hand on the gray of her gray,
and she leads me through empty spaces.

You move and push and like to imagine
that your sound is not like the sound of stone on stone;
however, you are wrong: I am the only one
who lives and suffers and has a sound.
I have an endless scream in me,
and I don't know which is screaming, my heart
or my intestines.

Do you recognize my songs? You didn't sing them,
not quite with the stressing I use.
Every morning new light comes
warmly into the open house,
and you have a feeling that moves from face to face,
and that leads you astray to caring.

Das Lied des Trinkers

Es war nicht in mir. Es ging aus und ein.
Da wollt ich es halten. Da hielt es der Wein.
(Ich weiss nicht mehr, was es war.)
Dann hielt er mir jenes und hielt mir dies,
bis ich mich ganz auf ihn verliess.
Ich Narr.

Jetzt bin ich in seinem Spiel, und er streut
mich verächtlich herum und verliert mich noch heut
an dieses Vieh, an den Tod.
Wenn der mich, schmutzige Karte, gewinnt,
so kratzt er mit mir seinen grauen Grind
und wirft mich fort in den Kot.

The Song the Drunkard Sings

It wasn't really inside me. It came in and went again.
I wanted to hold it. But the wine was holding it.
(I've forgotten now exactly what it was.)
Then he held this out to me, and that out to me,
till I was completely dependent on him.
I'm an ass.

Now I'm playing his game, and he throws me here and there,
wherever he pleases, and maybe today he'll lose
me to that pig, death.
When death has won me, the smudged-up card,
he will scratch his old scabs with me
and toss me on the heap.

Das Lied des Selbstmörders

Also noch einen Augenblick.
Dass sie mir immer wieder den Strick
zerschneiden.
Neulich war ich so gut bereit,
und es war schon ein wenig Ewigkeit
in meinen Eingeweiden.

Halten sie mir den Löffel her,
diesen löffel Leben.
Nein, ich will und ich will nicht mehr,
lasst mich mich übergeben.

Ich weiss, das Leben ist gar und gut,
und die Welt ist ein voller Topf,
aber mir geht es nicht ins Blut,
mir steigt es nur zu Kopf.

Andere nährt es, mich macht es krank;
begreift, dass man's verschmäht.
Mindestens ein Jahrtausend lang
brauch ich jetzt Diät.

The Song the Suicide Sings

Just another moment left!
But what they're doing to me, they're always taking the rope
and cutting it!
The other day it was so good!
And there was already a little bit of eternity
in my intestines.

They hold this spoon out to me,
this spoon of life.
Well, I want it, and I don't.
I'd better throw up.

I know that life is just fantastic fun,
and the world is a foamy mug;
but I don't really get strength from it,
it just makes me dizzy.

It heals others, it makes me sick.
Grasp that some can't stand it.
For at least a thousand years now
I'll have to fast.

Das Lied der Witwe

Am Anfang war mir das Leben gut.
Es hielt mich warm, es machte mir Mut.
Dass es das allen Jungen tut,
wie konnt ich das damals wissen.
Ich wusste nicht, was das Leben war—,
auf einmal war es nur Jahr und Jahr,
nicht mehr gut, nicht mehr neu, nicht mehr wunderbar,
wie mitten entzwei gerissen.

Das war nicht seine, nicht meine Schuld;
wir hatten beide nichts als Geduld,
aber der Tod hat keine.
Ich sah ihn kommen (wie schlecht er kam),
und ich schaute ihm zu, wie er nahm und nahm:
es war ja gar nicht das Meine.

Was war denn das Meine; Meines, Mein?
War mir nicht selbst mein Elendsein
nur vom Schicksal geliehn?
Das Schicksal will nicht nur das Glück,
es will die Pein und das Schrein zurück,
und es kauft für alt den Ruin.

Das Schicksal war da und erwarb für ein Nichts
jeden Ausdruck meines Gesichts
bis auf die Art zu gehn.
Das war ein täglicher Ausverkauf,
und als ich leer war, gab es mich auf
und liess mich offen stehn.

The Song the Widow Sings

At first life was good to me.
It kept me warm, it gave me courage.
Of course it does that to all the young,
but how could I have known that?
I had no idea what life was—
suddenly it was nothing but year after year,
not good anymore, not fresh anymore, not wonderful
                                                anymore,
as if torn in two pieces down the center.

It wasn't his fault, and it wasn't mine;
neither of us had much except patience,
and death didn't have any.
I saw him come (what an ugly sight),
and I watched him, while he took and took:
of course what he took wasn't mine.

What did belong to me then, what did I have that was mine?
Wasn't even my grief
only a loan from Fate?
Fate wants not only the happiness,
he wants the pain and the screaming back,
and he buys it all secondhand.

Fate was there and got for almost nothing
every expression on my face,
everything except the way I walk.
Every day he had a clearance sale,
and when I was empty, he walked out
and left the door open.

Das Lied des Idioten

Sie hindern mich nicht. Sie lassen mich gehn.
Sie sagen, es könne nichts geschehn.
Wie gut.
Es kann nichts geschehn. Alles kommt und kreist
immerfort um den Heiligen Geist,
um den gewissen Geist (du weisst)—,
wie gut.

Nein, man muss wirklich nicht meinen, es sei
irgend eine Gefahr dabei.
Das ist freilich das Blut.
Das Blut ist das Schwerste. Das Blut ist schwer.
Manchmal glaub ich, ich kann nicht mehr—.
(Wie gut.)

Ah, was ist das für ein schöner Ball;
rot und rund wie ein Überall.
Gut, dass ihr ihn erschuft.
Ob der wohl kommt, wenn man ruft?

Wie sich das alles seltsam benimmt,
ineinandertreibt, auseinanderschwimmt:
freundlich, ein wenig unbestimmt.
Wie gut.

The Song the Idiot Sings

They don't bother about me. They let me be.
They say, "Nothing can happen."
That's good.
Nothing *can* happen. It all comes and wheels
steadily around the Holy Ghost,
always around that same Ghost (you know)—
that's good.

No, of course not, one mustn't think any *danger*
could come in that way.
Of course the blood exists.
Blood is the heaviest. Blood is heavy.
Sometimes I think I've had too much.
(That's good.)

Oh, isn't that a wonderful ball!
round and red as nothing and all.
Good thing that you created it.
But will it come if you call?

How strangely this whole thing behaves,
into each other driving, out of each other swimming,
friendly, a touch uncertain.
That's good.

Das Lied der Waise

Ich bin Niemand und werde auch Niemand sein.
Jetzt bin ich ja zum Sein noch zu klein;
aber auch später.

Mütter und Väter,
erbarmt euch mein.

Zwar es lohnt nicht des Pflegens Müh:
ich werde doch gemäht.
Mich kann keiner brauchen: jetzt ist es zu früh
und morgen ist es zu spät.

Ich habe nur dieses eine Kleid,
es wird dünn und es verbleicht,
aber es hält eine Ewigkeit
auch noch vor Gott vielleicht.

Ich habe nur dieses bisschen Haar
(immer dasselbe blieb),
das einmal Eines Liebstes war.

Nun hat er nichts mehr lieb.

The Song the Orphan Sings

I am nobody, and I will be nobody too.
Now I'm too small to live, of course:
later it'll be the same.

Mothers and fathers,
think of me.

Of course it isn't worth the trouble of raising me:
I will be mowed down anyway.
Nobody can use me: it's too early now;
tomorrow, too late!

I have only this one dress,
and it's getting thin and bleached;
however, it will last an eternity
in the eyes of God.

I just have these few locks of hair
(they never change) that once
somebody loved.

Now he is through with love.

Das Lied des Zwerges

Meine Seele ist vielleicht grad und gut;
aber mein Herz, mein verbogenes Blut,
alles das, was mir wehe tut,
kann sie nicht aufrecht tragen.
Sie hat keinen Garten, sie hat kein Bett,
sie hängt an meinem scharfen Skelett
mit entsetztem Flügelschlagen.

Aus meinen Händen wird auch nichts mehr.
Wie verkümmert sie sind: sieh her:
zähe hüpfen sie, feucht und schwer,
wie kleine Kröten nach Regen.
Und das Andere an mir ist
abgetragen und alt und trist;
warum zögert Gott, auf den Mist
alles das hinzulegen.

Ob er mir zürnt für mein Gesicht
mit dem mürrischen Munde?
Es war ja so oft bereit, ganz licht
und klar zu werden im Grunde;
aber nichts kam ihm je so dicht
wie die grossen Hunde.
Und die Hunde haben das nicht.

———

The Song the Dwarf Sings

It's possible my soul is upright and O.K.;
but it can't make my heart stand straight
or my crooked blood—it's from those things
that the pain comes.
My soul has no place to walk in, no place to lie,
it catches onto my sharp skeleton
with a terrified beating of wings.

My hands will never amount to anything either.
See how stunted they are?
They're moist, they hop around sluggishly
like toads after a rain.
And everything else in me
is sad and old and worn out;
why does God hesitate to throw it all out
on the dump?

Is he angry with me, perhaps, for my face
with its sullen mouth?
It was ready, so often, to be full
of light and clear deep through;
but nothing ever came as close to it
as the big dogs did.
And dogs don't have it.

Das Lied des Aussätzigen

Sieh, ich bin einer, den alles verlassen hat.
Keiner weiss in der Stadt von mir,
Aussatz hat mich befallen.
Und ich schlage mein Klapperwerk,
klopfe mein trauriges Augenmerk
in die Ohren allen,
die nahe vorübergehn.
Und die es hölzern hören, sehn
erst gar nicht her, und was hier geschehn,
wollen sie nicht erfahren.

Soweit der Klang meiner Klapper reicht,
bin ich zuhause; aber vielleicht
machst du meine Klapper so laut,
dass sich keiner in meine Ferne traut,
der mir jetzt aus der Nähe weicht,
So dass ich sehr lange gehen kann,
ohne Mädchen, Frau oder Mann
oder Kind zu entdecken.

Tiere will ich nicht schrecken.

The Song the Leper Sings

I am one of those people whom everything has given up.
Nobody in the city knows that I exist.
Leprosy has happened to me.
And I strike my wooden clapper,
knock my sad theme song
into the ear of every person
who comes near.
And those who hear that sound look
certainly not here, and what is happening here
they don't care to know.

As far as the sound of my clapper reaches, there
I am at home; but maybe
you're making my clapper so loud
that they won't trust my distance any more
than they trust my nearness now.
I'm able to go a very long way
without coming on girl, woman,
child, or man.

But it bothers me when I frighten animals.

FROM New Poems

(*Neue Gedichte*)

1903–1908

In September of 1905, Rodin offered Rilke a job as his secretary. Rilke accepted, moved to Meudon, and by doing so, brought himself into a strong friendship with Rodin. Rodin taught him a great deal. For an artist, Rodin said, the thing is not dreaming, or talking, but work. "Travailler, travailler, travailler!" he shouted once, trying to explain how new works came to him. When Rilke confided one day that he hadn't been writing lately, Rodin did not adivse him to change diet or find a new relationship; he suggested that Rilke go to the zoo. What shall I do there? Look at an animal until you see it. Two or three weeks might not be too long. Rilke chose a panther; and wrote the first of his "seeing" poems, the famous poem which imitates in its sound the panther's walk. Rilke's letters mention a small and ancient sculpture of a panther which Rodin owned, on which he also practiced his seeing. Rilke sensed something new in this panther poem, and though he finished it before the *The Book of Pictures* was published, he saved it, to see what other poems might come to join it.

Rilke's early poetry did not satisfy him; he felt many of the poems were vague, poetic, and talky. His dissatisfaction led to a massive effort, which I've mentioned, to make the poems in *The Book of Pictures* blocky and weighty, with human shapes in them. His poems by 1906 had a marvelous solidity, but with Rodin's help he was about to enter a new area. He was about to ask an object a question and then listen. As Antonio Machado said:

> To talk with someone,
> ask a question first . . .
> then, listen.

In *The Book of Pictures* Rilke still wrote often from personal memory—the poem about his mother and himself is an example—or from historical memory: the poems about Karl the Twelfth or the Last Supper are examples. Memory offered its mysterious substance, unseen by the physical eye, and then the poet made sure by vivid images that we could see it.

Through Rodin's example and words, Rilke began to think that seeing may be something quite different from what he had been doing. Other poets have practiced seeing. Goethe observed plants meticulously with scientific method, and this labor seemed to feed his oceanic, passionate poems, to fill them with inward intensity. Goethe respected the discipline of seeing. Novalis, slightly younger than Goethe, wrote an aphorism in 1800 and declared that there are two natural stages in an artist's life. During the first stage the artist goes inward, to *Innigkeit*, exclusive contemplation of the self, a stage that may last years. But if an artist stays there, he or she has gone only halfway, because the second stage, according to Novalis, involves a "sober and spontaneous" observation of the outer world. Putting "sober" and "spontaneous" next to each other is wonderful. Both adjectives are apt for Dürer's crab or his clump of marsh grass or his rabbit; both apply to the meticulous detail Chinese artists influenced by Buddhism brought into their paintings. It's as if there was some spiritual force that leaves our body through the eyes, spontaneously pulled out, and this force or being gets stronger precisely by being out there, seeing what is not us. It gets stronger because there is something that responds. Walter Spink has called attention to the old Chinese statement "When a question is posed ceremoniously, the universe responds."

The living master of the "seeing" poem is Francis Ponge. His poems on "The Orange," "The Oyster," "The End of Autumn," "The Pleasures of the Door," are masterpieces. Ponge declares that the seeing poem represents a new kind of literature, which goes beyond the categories "Romantic" and "Classical." It does this by "the primacy accorded to matter, to the object, to the unbelievable qualities that emerge from it." "Nothing can prevent the meanings which have been locked into the simplest object or person from always striking the hour. . . . In these terms, one will surely understand what I consider to be the function of poetry. It is to nourish the spirit of man by giving him the cosmos to suckle."

Rilke now gave himself to the discipline of Novalis's "second stage." He worked fiercely, intensely on the object, even listing objects not yet written about, and checking them off when he had finished his poem about them. The list still exists. All this work he saw as new, and he gave the title *Neue Gedichte* to his next collection. He wrote over two hundred of these poems working many hours a day, from 1903 to 1908. Not all the poems in *New Poems* center on objects, but all involve concentrated seeing. "The Panther" and "The Swan" are strong examples of the seeing power. We are at a disadvantage reading the poems in translation, because Rilke's raft movement into the object is carried by the sound as it flows from one vowel to another. He uses sound in an ingenious, humorous, and sober way. Even those who do not know German can hear, if they read over the four opening lines of "The Panther" the *ä* sound, repeating, returning monotonously, incessantly, like the bars before the panther's eyes.

> *Sein Blick ist vom Vorübergehn der Stäbe*
> *so müd geworden, dass er nichts mehr hält.*
> *Ihm ist, als ob es tausend Stäbe gäbe*
> *und hinter tausend Stäben keine Welt.*

In "The Swan," Rilke says that our lives are clumsy because we have to move constantly through what we haven't yet accomplished.

> *This clumsy living that moves lumbering*
> *as if in ropes through what is not done*
> *reminds us of the awkward way the swan walks.*

The German line waddles:

> *Diese Mühsal, durch noch Ungetanes*
> *schwer und wie gebunden hinzugehn,*
> *gleicht dem ungeschaffnen Gang des Schwanes.*

In the third stanza, the swan slips into the water. Rilke brings the swan's sailing into an eerie association with death; now the German changes and begins to sail. The motion itself becomes a thing. "Another way of approaching the thing is to consider it unnamed, unnameable," Ponge said.

Rilke wrote a poem on an old Roman road he knew well, lined with gravestones and tombs; the sound in German becomes nervous, tight, even hysterical. The road possesses some sort of nonhuman intelligence, which gives and receives "emptiness."

> . . . *he lifts in a pitiful*
> *way his empty places up to the sky,*
> *looking around quickly, if any window*
> *is peeking. And while he waves*
>
> *the broad aqueducts to come on,*
> *the sky takes up his offer and gives him*
> *its empty places, which are longer lived.*

His sound is once more crucial in the poem on the swan's lovemaking with Leda. I consider this poem a masterpiece several times over. Many poets have written on Leda and the Swan. With his work on seeing guiding him, Rilke writes not as a man interested in myth but as a person interested in the sensual experience of the swan during the lovemaking. A surprising union takes place at the end, not of human being and myth, as in Yeats's brilliant poem, nor of woman and lover, but of the god and his feathers.

I've mentioned Rilke's love of sculpture; it was a force throughout his life. One is not surprised that he would write several of his seeing poems on statues, and I've included two of them. The Apollo statue, a headless torso, he saw again and again in the Louvre, where it has the title "Torso of a Youth from Miletus." There's a good photograph of it in the booklet called "The Visual Arts and Rilke's Poetry," published by the German Department at the University of Kansas (1978). Rilke's view of Apollo is startling, particularly in 1906, for its emphasis on Apollo's sexuality. Europe in general always took Apollo to be the god of rationality; recent speculation by Lopez-Pedraza and others sees Apollo as an energy linked to Dionysus and Hermes, much wilder and darker than "reason." Rilke's power of seeing pulled Apollo's dark side right out of the stone, before this side was known to Western students. Rilke emphasizes the animal nature of Apollo's body, and its sexual center. He draws from that concentrated study, that sensual experience of the eyes, one sentence: "You must change your life."

Apparently Rodin kept the Buddha statue in his garden at Meudon, a seated Buddha, with a golden oval shape around the head, suggesting developed spiritual light. Through looking at the oval, Rilke arrived at the almond.

> *The core of every core, the kernel of every kernel,*
> *an almond! held in itself, deepening in sweetness:*
> *all of this, everything, right up to the stars,*
> *is the meat around your stone. Accept my bow.*
>
> *Oh, yes, you feel it, how the weights on you are gone!*
> *Your husk has reached into what has no end,*
> *and that is where the great saps are brewing now.*
> *On the outside a warmth is helping,*
>
> *for, high, high above, your own suns are growing*
> *immense and they glow as they wheel around.*
> *Yet something has already started to live*
> *in you that will live longer than the suns.*

Der Panther

Im Jardin des Plantes, Paris

Sein Blick ist vom Vorübergehn der Stäbe
so müd geworden, dass er nichts mehr hält.
Ihm ist, als ob es tausend Stäbe gäbe
und hinter tausend Stäben keine Welt.

Der weiche Gang geschmeidig starker Schritte,
der sich im allerkleinsten Kreise dreht,
ist wie ein Tanz von Kraft um eine Mitte,
in der betäubt ein grosser Wille steht.

Nur manchmal schiebt der Vorhang der Pupille
sich lautlos auf—. Dann geht ein Bild hinein,
geht durch der Glieder angespannte Stille—
und hört im Herzen auf zu sein.

The Panther

In the Jardin des Plantes, Paris

From seeing the bars, his seeing is so exhausted
that it no longer holds anything anymore.
To him the world is bars, a hundred thousand
bars, and behind the bars, nothing.

The lithe swinging of that rhythmical easy stride
which circles down to the tiniest hub
is like a dance of energy around a point
in which a great will stands stunned and numb.

Only at times the curtains of the pupil rise
without a sound . . . then a shape enters,
slips through the tightened silence of the shoulders,
reaches the heart, and dies.

Der Schwan

Diese Mühsal, durch noch Ungetanes
schwer und wie gebunden hinzugehn,
gleicht dem ungeschaffnen Gang des Schwanes.

Und das Sterben, dieses Nichtmehrfassen
jenes Grunds, auf dem wir täglich stehn,
seinem ängstlichen Sich-Niederlassen—:

in die Wasser, die ihn sanft empfangen
und die sich, wie glücklich und vergangen,
unter ihm zurückziehn, Flut um Flut;
während er unendlich still und sicher
immer mündiger und königlicher
und gelassener zu ziehn geruht.

The Swan

This clumsy living that moves lumbering
as if in ropes through what is not done
reminds us of the awkward way the swan walks.

And to die, which is a letting go
of the ground we stand on and cling to every day,
is like the swan when he nervously lets himself down

into the water, which receives him gaily
and which flows joyfully under
and after him, wave after wave,
while the swan, unmoving and marvelously calm,
is pleased to be carried, each minute more fully grown,
more like a king, composed, farther and farther on.

Römische Campagna

Aus der vollgestellten Stadt, die lieber
schliefe, träumend von den hohen Thermen,
geht der grade Gräberweg ins Fieber;
und die Fenster in den letzten Fermen

sehn ihm nach mit einem bösen Blick.
Und er hat sie immer im Genick,
wenn her hingeht, rechts und links zerstörend,
bis er draussen atemlos beschwörend

seine Leere zu den Himmeln hebt,
hastig um sich schauend, ob ihn keine
Fenster treffen. Während er den weiten

Aquädukten zuwinkt herzuschreiten,
geben ihm die Himmel für die seine
ihre Leere, die ihn überlebt.

Roman Countryside

Out of the overcrowded city, which would much rather
sleep anyway, dreaming of the aristocratic Springs,
the steep tomb road comes down feverishly;
and the windows that belong to the last farms

give the road a sinister look as it passes them.
These windows are just behind his back all the time
as he hurries on, destroying this way and that way,
until, out of the city, out of breath, he lifts in a pitiful

way his empty places up to the sky,
looking around quickly, if any window
is peeking. And while he waves

the broad aqueducts to come on,
the sky takes up his offer and gives him
its empty places, which are longer lived.

Leda

Als ihn der Gott in seiner Not betrat,
erschrak er fast, den Schwan so schön zu finden;
er liess sich ganz verwirrt in ihm verschwinden.
Schon aber trug ihn sein Betrug zur Tat,

bevor er noch des unerprobten Seins
Gefühle prüfte. Und die Aufgetane
erkannte schon den Kommenden im Schwane
und wusste schon: er bat um eins,

das sie, verwirrt in ihrem Widerstand,
nicht mehr verbergen konnte. Er kam nieder,
und halsend durch die immer schwächre Hand

liess sich der Gott in die Geliebte los.
Dann erst empfand er glücklich sein Gefieder
und wurde wirklich Schwan in ihrem Schooss.

Leda

When the god, needing something, decided to become a swan,
he was astounded how lovely the bird was;
he was dizzy as he disappeared into the swan.
But his deceiving act soon pulled him into the doing,

before he had a chance to test all the new feelings
inside the being. And the woman, open to him,
recognized the One Soon To Be in the swan
and she knew: what he asked for

was something which, confused in her defending, she
could no longer keep from him. He pressed closer
and pushing his neck through her less and less firm hand

let the god loose into the darling woman.
Then for the first time he found his feathers marvelous
and lying in her soft place he became a swan.

Archaïscher Torso Apollos

Wir kannten nicht sein unerhörtes Haupt,
darin die Augenäpfel reiften. Aber
sein Torso glüht noch wie ein Kandelaber,
in dem sein Schauen, nur zurückgeschraubt,

sich hält und glänzt. Sonst könnte nicht der Bug
der Brust dich blenden, und im leisen Drehen
der Lenden Könnte nicht ein Lächeln gehen
zu jener Mitte, die die Zeugung trug.

Sonst stünde dieser Stein entstellt und kurz
unter der Schultern durchsichtigem Sturz
und flimmerte nicht so wie Raubtierfelle;

und bräche nicht aus allen seinen Rändern
aus wie ein Stern: denn da ist keine Stelle,
die dich nicht sieht. Du musst dein Leben ändern.

Archaic Torso of Apollo

We have no idea what his fantastic head
was like, where the eyeballs were slowly swelling. But
his body now is glowing like a gas lamp,
whose inner eyes, only turned down a little,

hold their flame, shine. If there weren't light, the curve
of the breast wouldn't blind you, and in the swerve
of the thighs a smile wouldn't keep on going
toward the place where the seeds are.

If there weren't light, this stone would look cut off
where it drops clearly from the shoulders,
its skin wouldn't gleam like the fur of a wild animal,

and the body wouldn't send out light from every edge
as a star does . . . for there is no place at all
that isn't looking at you. You must change your life.

Der Einsame

Nein: ein Turm soll sein aus meinem Herzen
und ich selbst an seinen Rand gestellt:
wo sonst nichts mehr ist, noch einmal Schmerzen
und Unsäglichkeit, noch einmal Welt.

Noch ein Ding allein im Übergrossen,
welches dunkel wird und wieder licht,
noch ein letztes, sehnendes Gesicht,
in das Nie-zu-Stillende verstossen,

noch ein äusserstes Gesicht aus Stein,
willig seinen inneren Gewichten,
das die Weiten, die es still vernichten,
zwingen, immer seliger zu sein.

The Solitary Man

No, what my heart will be is a tower,
and I will be right out on its rim:
nothing else will be there, only pain
and what can't be said, only the world.

Only one thing left in the enormous space
that will go dark and then light again,
only one final face full of longing,
exiled into what is always full of thirst,

only one farthest-out face made of stone,
at peace with its own inner weight,
which the distances, who go on ruining it,
force on to deeper holiness.

Buddha in der Glorie

Mitte aller Mitten, Kern der Kerne,
Mandel, die sich einschliesst und versüsst,—
dieses alles bis an alle Sterne
ist dein Fruchtfleisch: Sei gegrüsst.

Sieh, du fühlst, wie nichts mehr an dir hängt;
im Unendlichen ist deine Schale,
und dort steht der starke Saft und drängt.
Und von aussen hilft ihm ein Gestrahle,

denn ganz oben werden deine Sonnen
voll und glühend umgedreht.
Doch in dir ist schon begonnen,
was die Sonnen übersteht.

Buddha Inside the Light

The core of every core, the kernel of every kernel,
an almond! held in itself, deepening in sweetness:
all of this, everything, right up to the stars,
is the meat around your stone. Accept my bow.

Oh, yes, you feel it, how the weights on you are gone!
Your husk has reached into what has no end,
and that is where the great saps are brewing now.
On the outside a warmth is helping,

for, high, high above, your own suns are growing
immense and they glow as they wheel around.
Yet something has already started to live
in you that will live longer than the suns.

FROM The Uncollected

and Occasional Poems

1914–1926

A NEW BOOK by Rilke, as the reader will realize by now, did not mean merely a new collection but a new stage. A new stage was slow in coming after the publication of the "seeing" poems in 1908, perhaps because of the war tension in 1914–1918. (The German army drafted Rilke, and he served as an archivist in Vienna during 1916.) There were other reasons. From 1908, when he published the enlarged second edition of *Neue Gedichte*, until 1923, when he published the *Duino Elegies* and the *Sonnets to Orpheus*, no important collection appeared. Rilke waited with patience for fifteen years. He published a cycle on the Virgin Mary in 1913, but he considered this to be an occasional poem.

It wasn't that he wrote no poetry during those years. He continued to write, and many of the poems were magnificent. But he had set his heart on a new departure, something deep and amazing that would justify his life, and it didn't happen. He didn't want occasional poems; he wanted something intense, fierce: a single work, a unified creation. As it turned out, he received two such works, at almost the same time. But in the meantime he wrote the group of poems I'm giving a sample of here. The poems are not well known because Rilke did not honor them by putting them in a book, and also because some have not been available in English, and finally because the official English translator chosen by the Rilke estate was J. B. Leishman, whose translations are so bad one sometimes can't figure out what the subject of a poem is. Leishman's translations have been a great frustration to everyone, and only now that Rilke's work is in the public domain can other translations come out.

Between the "seeing poems," then, and the waterfalls of feeling called the *Duino Elegies* and the *Sonnets*, there are the scattered or uncollected poems. Rilke wrote over two hundred ungathered poems during the last twenty years of his life. Also, many occasional poems have been found, in flyleafs or guestbooks, or composed spontaneously in letters. Some of the occasional poems are very fine, especially those he and Erika Mitterer exchanged in lieu of letters. Many treasures are waiting there for good translators.

After 1908, some of Rilke's certainties disappeared; his life lost some forward drive. He felt exhausted after *Neue Gedichte* and *Malte Laurids Brigge.* Europe itself seemed to falter. The European psyche had created with astounding intensity through the whole nineteenth century, throwing out indefatigable empire soldiers, fierce industrialists, energetic inventors, ingenious linguistic students, serious archaeologists, exciting philosophical speculators, and psychological geniuses such as Janet, Bleuler, and Fechner. The peak was around 1888–1889. About 1908, Europe began to falter, and in 1914 it committed suicide. Eliot, Pound, and Graves did not inherit the abundant high-spirited thought energy of Europe, as did Rilke, born only a few years earlier, but rather the flat death energy hidden inside the abundance. So we can expect despair in Rilke's poems after 1914, as he watched his inheritance, that tremendous human energy, collapse.

> *Heart, whom will you cry out to? More and more alone,*
> *you make your way through the ununderstandable*
> *human beings. All the more hopeless perhaps*
> *since it holds to its old course,*
> *the course toward the future,*
> *that's lost.*
>
> *Happened before. Did you mourn? What was it? A fallen*
> *berry of joy, still green.*
> *But now my oak of joy is breaking,*
> *what is breaking in storm is my slowly*
> *grown oak of joy.*

Rilke wrote in August of 1914 a small group of poems welcoming the "war god." He was later ashamed of them. His regret for that contagion slowed his work. When he did write, he looked at what was missing in his first book: his losses.

In 1914 he also decided he had done enough visualization work. What he had not done was heart work. He wrote a poem that year called *"Wendung,"* which can be "Crisis" or "Turning." Michael Hamburger has a good translation of it in his *Modern German Poetry 1910–1950.*

Work of seeing is done,
now practise heart-work
upon those images captive within you . . .

In his letters he blames himself for coldness, for being unable
to give himself as others do, especially as the great women lovers
he had read of, Gaspara Stampa and Marianne Alcoforado, had
done. Why couldn't he do that? He thought some of his coldness
came from his mother's conventionality and he blamed her.

But also he and Clara throughout their lives had put their
obligation to art above their human obligations. They saw their
road as heroic, the intense, the noble one. The clarity with which
they saw it was Europe's great gift to them. Their daughter,
Ruth, came second. They gave up trying to live together after
1902 or so. Ruth sometimes stayed with her mother in the studio,
sometimes with her grandmother. The dedication to art finally
took the form of a vivid, unforgettable detail. Rilke did not go
to his daughter's wedding for fear of losing his concentration.
This seems too heroic to me, but the whole tradition has been
virtually lost in the United States, so it is difficult to judge.

The life without heart no longer satisfied him. He wrote aston-
ishing letters, pledging eternal love, to women he had never met.
His poems, he said, contained secret mating calls; one woman
who heard that call was the superb pianist Magda von Hatting-
berg, whom he called "Benvenuta." After corresponding pas-
sionately for several months, they decided to meet; but the meeting
didn't seem to bear out the feeling in the correspondence. Her
intelligence and feeling were immense, and the two became deep
friends; but the fall from the earlier height made it clear to him
that something was wrong, either his ideas of relationship ("each
person protecting the solitude of the other") or his ability to
love a human being.

A few of the ungathered poems show him struggling against
his old Romantic idealization of women. One of them is "We
Must Die Because We Have Known Them," from 1914, in which
he adopts a saying from ancient Egypt to throw some dark light
on his fear of women. The poem is well balanced, and brilliant
in its images. The enthusiastic "anima" moods of adolescence,
as Jung would call them, are compared to the adult male's more

calm awareness of danger. He faces this fear clearly, and doesn't try to explain it, or give cultural reasons for it.

The ungathered poems in general leave the highly disciplined, chiseled technique of the seeing poems, and take on the mood of water. The lines are often uneven in length, the associations swift. Rilke moves more and more like Hermes each year, flying swiftly into the invisible and back. The poem "Left Out to Die" is not written for a reader who needs to be led by the hand through a poem. Rilke follows intuitive paths, doesn't look back, and strides surely along.

> *Left out to die on the mountains of the heart. Look,*
> *   how tiny it is,*
> *do you see: the final barn of language, and, above it,*
> *still tiny, one final*
> *granary of feeling. You've seen it before?*
> *Left out to die on the mountains of the heart.*

Because the poem is so powerfully intuitive, it is difficult to comment on the lines without diminishing their mystery. We know the machine civilization shrivels Eros, and that diminishing surely lies under this poem. But is this fear in the heart an experience peculiar to writers and intellectuals? They leave the unconsciousness of popular culture, its unconscious sociability, and spend their lives trying to increase their store of consciousness. The poem moves through material similar to what Edmund Wilson explored in *The Wound and the Bow* and Thomas Mann in *Death in Venice.* Why is it that a person of sensibility in Western culture so often does not conclude in a joyful old age?

> *Many goats and deer go here, their knowing whole,*
> *many surefooted mountain animals*
> *change grass or stay. And the big cared-for bird*
> *circles around the pure refusal of the peaks. But*
> *not cared for, here on the mountains of the heart . . .*

The large protected bird retains his mystery, circling around the *Verweigerung* of the peaks. That *Verweigerung*—literally "denial"—could be an eternal nay-saying, or self-denial, or even asceticism.

I suppose the most astonishing of these late poems are about music and about the hand. In both, the concentration learned in the seeing poems reappears, now concentrated on feelings shared with others. He doesn't say, "I like music"; in fact, the word "I" never appears in "On Music" at all. But he hears, and hears what others hear. Astonishing transformations take place in the poem: ears turn to eyes, music turns into a "countryside we can hear." He suggests that in Bach's music, for example, the deepest, most interior thing in us suddenly appears out there, as amazing space, as "the other side of the air."

His hand poem I find astonishing too. His longing to take the hands of others deepened, I think, as he grew older, and two years before he died, he wrote "Palm." The roads in the palm walk themselves, he says; that is, the lines in our palm alter according to our experiences. A beautiful detail appears: we notice the hills of our own palm only when it meets another person's. Entering another person's hand resembles traveling through a countryside; when we arrive at the other palm, we fill it, as a train station is filled with a train, with the joy of having arrived.

As he gets older, Rilke urges poets again and again to train their imagination like a body, to aim and struggle for something intense. Being carried along, drifting, is not enough. He wants them to reach far out, not to be so lazy, to labor.

> *To work with things is not hubris*
> *when building the association beyond words;*
> *denser and denser the pattern becomes—*
> *being carried along is not enough.*

He imagines vast associations, the intricate harmony the Renaissance thinkers guessed at, the dream that each particle knows of every other particle, and even knows that we are observing it. To do nothing in such a world implies, as Rumi says, that "no gifts have been given."

> *Take your well-disciplined strengths*
> *and stretch them between two*
> *opposing poles. Because inside human beings*
> *is where God learns.*

»Man Muss Sterben Weil Man Sie Kennt«

(»Papyrus Prisse«. Aus den Sprüchen des Ptah-hetep,
Handschrift um 2000 v. Ch.)

»Man muss sterben weil man sie kennt.« Sterben
an der unsäglichen Blüte des Lächelns. Sterben
an ihren leichten Händen. Sterben
an Frauen.

Singe der Jüngling die tödlichen,
wenn sie ihm hoch durch den Herzraum
wandeln. Aus seiner blühenden Brust
sing er sie an:
unerreichbare! Ach, wie sie fremd sind.
Über den Gipfeln
seines Gefühls gehn sie hervor und ergiessen
süss verwandelte Nacht ins verlassene
Tal seiner Arme. Es rauscht
Wind ihres Aufgangs im Laub seines Leibes. Es glänzen
seine Bäche dahin.

Aber der Mann
schweige erschütterter. Er, der
pfadlos die Nacht im Gebirg
seiner Gefühle geirrt hat:
schweige.

Wie der Seemann schweigt, der ältere,
und die bestandenen
Schrecken spielen in ihm wie in zitternden Käfigen.

"We Must Die Because We Have Known Them"

(Papyrus Prisse. From the sayings
of Ptah-hotep, manuscript from 2000 B.C.)

"We must die because we have known them." Die
of the unbelievable flower of their smile. Die
of their delicate hands. Die of women.

The adolescent boy praises the death-givers,
when they float magnificently through his
heart halls. From his blossoming body
he cries out to them:
impossible to reach. Oh, how strange they are.
They go swiftly over
the peaks of his emotions and pour down
the marvelously altered night into his deserted
arm valley. The wind that rises
in their dawn makes his body leaves rustle. His brooks
glisten away in the sun.

But the grown man
shivers and says nothing. The man
who has blundered around all night
on the mountains of his feelings remains
silent.

As the old sailor remains silent,
and the terrors
he's experienced leap about in him as if in rocking cages.

Paris, July 1914

Klage

Wem willst du klagen, Herz? Immer gemiedener
ringt sich dein Weg durch die unbegreiflichen
Menschen. Mehr noch vergebens vielleicht,
da er die Richtung behält,
Richtung zur Zukunft behält,
zu der verlorenen.

Früher. Klagtest? Was wars? Eine gefallene
Beere des Jubels, unreife.
Jetzt aber bricht mir mein Jubel-Baum,
bricht mir im Sturme mein langsamer
Jubel-Baum.
Schönster in meiner unsichtbaren
Landschaft, der du mich kenntlicher
machtest Engeln, unsichtbaren.

Mourning

Heart, whom will you cry out to? More and more alone,
you make your way through the unknowable
human beings. All the more hopeless perhaps
since it holds to its old course,
the course toward the future,
that's lost.

Happened before. Did you mourn? What was it? A fallen
berry of joy, still green.
But now my oak of joy is breaking,
what is breaking in storm is my slowly
grown oak of joy.
The loveliest thing in my invisible
landscape, helping me to be seen
by angels, that are invisible.

Paris, July 1914

163

Ausgesetzt auf den Bergen des Herzens

Ausgesetzt auf den Bergen des Herzens. Siehe, wie
                                  klein dort,
siehe: die letzte Ortschaft der Worte, und höher,
aber wie klein auch, noch ein letztes
Gehöft von Gefühl. Erkennst du's?
Ausgesetzt auf den Bergen des Herzens. Steingrund
unter den Händen. Hier blüht wohl
einiges auf; aus stummem Absturz
blüht ein unwissendes Kraut singend hervor.
Aber der Wissende? Ach, der zu wissen begann
und schweigt nun, ausgesetzt auf den Bergen des
                                  Herzens.
Da geht wohl, heilen Bewusstseins,
manches umher, manches gesicherte Bergtier,
wechselt und weilt. Und der grosse geborgene Vogel
kreist um der Gipfel reine Verweigerung.—Aber
ungeborgen, hier auf den Bergen des Herzens. . . .

Left Out to Die

Left out to die on the mountains of the heart. Look, how
                                                tiny it is,
do you see: the final barn of language, and, above it,
still tiny, one final
granary of feeling. You've seen it before?
Left out to die on the mountains of the heart. Hard stone
under the hands. True, something blooms
even here: an ignorant sprig blossoms
out singing from the dumb mountain steep.
But the man of consciousness? Ah, he began to be conscious
and then fell silent, left out to die on the heart mountains.
Many goats and deer go here, their knowing whole,
many surefooted mountain animals
change grass or stay. And the big cared-for bird
circles around the pure refusal of the peaks. But
not cared for, here on the mountains of the heart . . .

Irschenhausen, September 20, 1914

Immer wieder

Immer wieder, ob wir der Liebe Landschaft auch kennen
und den kleinen Kirchhof mit seinen klagenden Namen
und die furchtbar verschweigende Schlucht, in welcher die andern
enden: immer wieder gehn wir zu zweien hinaus
unter die alten Bäume, lagern uns immer wieder
zwischen die Blumen, gegenüber dem Himmel.

Again, Again!

Again, again, even if we know the countryside of love,
and the tiny churchyard with its names mourning,
and the chasm, more and more silent, terrifying, into which
                      the others
dropped: we walk out together anyway
beneath the ancient trees, we lie down again,
again, among the flowers, and face the sky.

Close of 1914

An die Musik

Musik: Atem der Statuen. Vielleicht:
Stille der Bilder. Du Sprache wo Sprachen
enden. Du Zeit,
die senkrecht steht auf der Richtung
                    vergehender Herzen.

Gefühle zu wem? O du der Gefühle
Wandlung in was?—: in hörbare Landschaft.
Du Fremde: Musik. Du uns entwachsener
Herzraum. Innigstes unser,
das, uns übersteigend, hinausdrängt,—
heiliger Abschied:
da uns das Innre umsteht
als geübteste Ferne, als andre
Seite der Luft:
rein,
riesig,
nicht mehr bewohnbar.

On Music

Music: the breathing of statues. Perhaps:
the silence of paintings. Language where
language ends. Time
that stands head-up in the direction
            of hearts that wear out.

Feeling . . . for whom? Place where feeling is
transformed . . . into what? Into a countryside we can hear.
Music: you stranger. You feeling space, growing
away from us. The deepest thing in us, that,
rising above us, forces its way out . . .
a holy goodbye:
when the innermost point in us stands
outside, as amazing space, as the other
side of the air:
pure,
immense,
not for us to live in now.

Munich, January 1918

Imaginärer Lebenslauf

Erst eine Kindheit, grenzenlos und ohne
Verzicht und Ziel. O unbewusste Lust.
Auf einmal Schrecken, Schranke, Schule, Frohne
und Absturz in Versuchung und Verlust.

Trotz. Der Gebogene wird selber Bieger
und rächt an anderen, dass er erlag.
Geliebt, gefürchtet, Retter, Ringer, Sieger
und Überwinder, Schlag auf Schlag.

Und dann allein im Weiten, Leichten, Kalten.
Doch tief in der errichteten Gestalt
ein Atemholen nach dem Ersten, Alten . . .

Da stürzte Gott aus seinem Hinterhalt.

Imaginary Biography

First childhood, no limits, no renunciations,
no goals. Such unthinking joy.
Then abruptly terror, schoolrooms, boundaries, captivity,
and a plunge into temptation and deep loss.

Defiance. The one crushed will be the crusher now,
and he avenges his defeats on others.
Loved, feared, he rescues, wrestles, wins,
and overpowers others, slowly, act by act.

And then all alone in space, in lightness, in cold.
But deep in the shape he has made to stand erect
he takes a breath, as if reaching for the First, Primitive . . .

Then God explodes from his hiding place.

Schöneck, September 1923

Irrlichter

Wir haben einen alten Verkehr
mit den Lichtern im Moor.
Sie kommen mir wie Grosstanten vor . . .
Ich entdecke mehr und mehr

zwischen ihnen und mir den Familienzug,
den keine Gewalt unterdrückt:
diesen Schwung, diesen Sprung, diesen Ruck, diesen Bug,
der den andern nicht glückt.

Auch ich bin dort, wo die Wege nicht gehn,
im Schwaden, den mancher mied,
und ich habe mich oft verlöschen sehn
unter dem Augenlid.

Fox Fire

We have an old association
with the lights out on the moors.
I have the feeling they are great-aunts. . . .
More and more I notice between them

and me a kind of family resemblance
that no force can suppress:
a certain jump, a leaping, a turn, a curve—
others can't seem to do it.

I too live where there are no roads,
in the mist that turns most people back,
and I've seen myself often too
go out under my own eyelids.

Muzot, February 1924

Da dich das geflügelte Entzücken

Da dich das geflügelte Entzücken
über manchen frühen Abgrund trug,
baue jetzt der unerhörten Brücken
kühn berechenbaren Bug.

Wunder ist nicht nur im unerklärten
Überstehen der Gefahr;
erst in einer klaren reingewährten
Leistung wird das Wunder wunderbar.

Mitzuwirken ist nicht Überhebung
an dem unbeschreiblichen Bezug,
immer inniger wird die Verwebung,
nur Getragensein ist nicht genug.

Deine ausgeübten Kräfte spanne,
bis sie reichen, zwischen zwein
Widersprüchen . . . Denn im Manne
will der Gott beraten sein.

Just as the Winged Energy of Delight

Just as the winged energy of delight
carried you over many chasms early on,
now raise the daringly imagined arch
holding up the astounding bridges.

Miracle doesn't lie only in the amazing
living through and defeat of danger;
miracles become miracles in the clear
achievement that is earned.

To work with things is not hubris
when building the association beyond words;
denser and denser the pattern becomes—
being carried along is not enough.

Take your well-disciplined strengths
and stretch them between two
opposing poles. Because inside human beings
is where God learns.

Muzot, February 1924

Spaziergang

Schon ist mein Blick am Hügel, dem besonnten,
dem Wege, den ich kaum begann, voran.
So fasst uns das, was wir nicht fassen konnten,
voller Erscheinung, aus der Ferne an—

und wandelt uns, auch wenn wirs nicht erreichen,
in jenes, das wir, kaum es ahnend, sind;
ein Zeichen weht, erwidernd unserm Zeichen . . .
Wir aber spüren nur den Gegenwind.

A Walk

My eyes already touch the sunny hill,
going far ahead of the road I have begun.
So we are grasped by what we cannot grasp;
it has its inner light, even from a distance—

and changes us, even if we do not reach it,
into something else, which, hardly sensing it, we already are;
a gesture waves us on, answering our own wave . . .
but what we feel is the wind in our faces.

Muzot, March 1924

Handinneres

Innres der Hand. Sohle, die nicht mehr geht
als auf Gefühl. Die sich nach oben hält
und im Spiegel
himmlische Strassen empfängt, die selber
wandelnden.
Die gelernt hat, auf Wasser zu gehn,
wenn sie schöpft,
die auf den Brunnen geht,
aller Wege Verwandlerin.
Die auftritt in anderen Händen,
die ihresgleichen
zur Landschaft macht:
wandert und ankommt in ihnen,
sie anfüllt mit Ankunft.

Palm

Palm of the hand. Sole, that walks now
only on feeling. The hand turns over
and in its mirror
shows heavenly roads, that themselves are
walking.
It has learned to stroll on water
when it dips down,
walks on top of fountains,
causes all roads to fork.
It steps forward into another's hand,
changes its doubles
into a countryside,
travels into them and arrives,
fills them with having arrived.

Muzot, October 1924

Dreizehnte Antwort

Für Erika
zum Feste der Rühmung

Taube, die draussen blieb,   ausser dem Taubenschlag,
wider in Kreis und Haus,   einig der Nacht, dem Tag,
weiss sie die Heimlichkeit,   wenn sich der Einbezug
fremdester Schrecken schmiegt   in den gefühlten Flug.

Unter den Tauben, die   allergeschonteste,
niemals gefährdetste,   kennt nicht die Zärtlichkeit;
wiedererholtes Herz   ist das bewohnteste:
freier durch Widerruf   freut sich die Fähigkeit.

Über dem Nirgendssein   spannt sich das Überall!
Ach der geworfene,   ach der gewagte Ball,
füllt er die Hände nicht   anders mit Wiederkehr:
rein um sein Heimgewicht   ist er mehr.

Ragaz, am 24. August 1926

(From the exchange of letter poems with Erika Mitterer:
This is Rilke's thirteenth letter)

*For Erika
and the Praise Festival*

The dove that remained away   lived outside the dovehouse
housed and warmed again   joined with night and day,
knows the secretive thing   in which the taking in
of the deepest terrors nestles   into the flight of feeling.

The dove inside the dovehouse   the most cared for dove
never open to danger   does not know the tenderness;
the heart gained back   is the richest:
more free by its circle   talent becomes glad.

The universe arches   over what is without home!
The ball that was thrown   yes, the ball we dared,
doesn't it fill the hand   differently as it comes back?
It is heavier purely   from the weight of home.

Postmarked Ragaz, August 24, 1926

The First Ten *Sonnets to Orpheus*

(Die Sonette an Orpheus)

1923

I DECIDED not to include the *Elegies* in this collection. There were two reasons. The *Elegies* are the most accessible part in English of Rilke's work; they have been rendered by a surprising number of translators. Stephen Spender worked over the Leishman translation years ago, improving it vastly; MacIntyre did the *Elegies* for the University of California Press; Stephen Garney and Jay Wilson published a new version in 1972; both Al Poulin and David Young have published new versions since then. It is true that the sound of the *Elegies* has not yet been brought over into English. I'm not sure what that would require. Moreover, I'm not convinced that the *Elegies* are Rilke's great work. There's something about them that is admirable but not likable. When Rilke's friend Magda von Hattingberg heard Rilke read some of the early passages, she told him that she felt a hostility to life in them. She had always disliked his essay attacking dolls; and she concluded there was a force in him that wanted to destroy certain simple joys. Western culture often instills in its artists an anxious craving to create the monumental work. The *Elegies* are magnificent in theme and sound, but they feel almost too cultured, as if they belonged to the memory banks of Europe, and not to an uncertain person called Rilke. I sense that certain weaknesses Rilke grieved over in private have become triumphs in the massive music of the *Elegies*. *Sonnets to Orpheus* is the masterpiece of his late life, I think. I glimpse his swiftly appearing, swiftly disappearing, Hermes personality more clearly in these poems than anywhere else.

Rilke always felt that there was something sinister in him, a hankering that stories would turn out badly, that bodies in the Resurrection would stand up with worms; he felt a constant anger at Christian piety, which turns into a cold hostility toward Christ, a rage against Christ's "interference." He felt in his own personality a blackness, the weight that appears in *Malte Laurids Brigge,* so heavy that Rilke wasn't sure that he could get out from under that book and walk again.

Yet he had always believed that the greatest art includes praise, amounts to praise. "To praise is the whole thing!" That instinct to praise, so apparent and persistent in primitive poetry, in Pindar, in ancient China, in Persia, in Provence, became weakened in later Europe; poetry of praise became unfashionable, especially among twentieth-century poets. For years Rilke had wanted to praise, but he couldn't find the door to the mine. One day, in February of 1922, while strolling about Valais, he saw in a shopwindow an old sketch of Orpheus, which Cima da Conegliano had sketched in 1518. It showed Orpheus playing a flute, surrounded by animals, listening. Our complaints about life do not intrigue animals, so perhaps Orpheus was praising. Furthermore, Orpheus's ability to play so that animals could hear it was surely connected to his descent into the dark. The ancient world loved that scene: Orpheus is playing, surrounded by listening animals. A third element might be the listening.

Rilke had adopted the discipline of seeing: he spent years on that road. It occurred to him now that listening might be a road in itself. It might be a great road. Perhaps one of the strengths of the twentieth century is our ability to listen. And he opened the sonnets with speculation on what is happening to the ear.

Orpheus is singing! A tree inside the ear! . . .

Animals created by silence came forward from the clear
and relaxed forest where their lairs were,
and it turned out the reason they were so full of silence
was not cunning, and not terror,

it was listening. Growling, yelping, grunting now
seemed all nonsense to them.

We didn't always know how to listen. Learning to listen is a cultural gift.

And where before
there was hardly a shed where this listening could go,

a rough shelter put up out of brushy longings,
with an entrance gate whose poles were wobbly,
you created a temple for them deep inside their ears.

Certain artists do open a new space in the ear, so that we hear something we've never heard before; I suppose Bach belongs to that group, Rameau, Cervantes, Chaucer, Rumi, Vallejo.

The *Elegies* and *Sonnets* came, as Rilke's great work had always come, in rushes, in a flood. The first group of sonnets arrived fully formed, images and rhythm and rhymes in place. In fact, sitting at a window seat, writing, he would occasionally miss a rhyme, even though he was writing as fast as he could. He regarded the *Sonnets* and *Elegies* as a gift from outside himself.

This experience of inflooding becomes a part of the content of the sonnets. To return to the theme: if listening is a road, a road on which one can travel, and if one learns at last how to listen, then following the road downward should be easy. "A god can do it." But it isn't. When a fork appears, we're lost. The ancient Greeks sometimes built a small temple for Apollo at a crossroads, and Rilke mentions that; if a man or woman came to the crossroads, and didn't know which road to take, he or she could go inside the temple, meditate in silence, and find out which way to go.

> *A man is split. And where two roads intersect*
> *inside us, no one has built the Singer's Temple.*

Then we arrive at the problem of desire, desiring ecstasy, desiring salvation.

> *Writing poetry as we learn from you is not desiring,*
> *not wanting something that can ever be achieved.*

When a man or a woman is singing, or writing poems—in the ancient world they were identical—what is going on? True singing, Rilke says, does not involve the attempt to accomplish something, to become a better person, to achieve salvation, or to publish a book. Using the heavy syllable "ah," which can't be reproduced in translation, he says: *"Gesang ist Dasein."* The sounds are rooted and strong. If we translate the phrase literally as "Singing is being," the result is pitiful. The whole meaning is gone, because the vowels are too light. I compromised, saying, "To write poetry is to be alive." "For a god that's easy." Rilke, then, surprisingly to me, declares that the love poems one writes in one's twenties are not true "singing." There's something a bit mechanical in them, unearned, and maybe also they lack terror.

> *Yes, you are young, and you love, and the voice*
> *forces your mouth open—that is lovely, but learn*
>
> *to forget that breaking into song. It doesn't last.*
> *Real singing is a different movement of air.*
> *Air moving around nothing. A breathing in a god. A wind.*

Rilke not only announces a theme, he thinks about it. Into this one sonnet he pours enough ideas to keep the normal poet working for five years. Oversimplifying, one could say that each poet feels inside his or her poem, that is, contributes feeling; other poets contribute perceptions as well, or perceive. Still others feel and perceive and also think. Wallace Stevens is surely one of those. It is wonderful to watch Goethe think in a poem, or Rumi. Rilke's thinking, when it arrives, does not appear as an ironic conceit, which is an offshoot of logic. Rilke in fact warned young poets against irony; when they feel irony is "becoming too intimate," they should avoid it. "Try to get at the depth of things— that is one place irony never goes down to." Rilke wants the energy of thought, and doesn't find that it pushes out joy. Thinking brings new force into a poem, then, but it is risky, because if the reader finds an idea untrue, he rejects the whole poem. But in the eighth sonnet Rilke declares that grief doesn't belong in a poem unless praise has already been there. That idea, if adopted, would alter our poetry considerably. So Rilke takes the risk of thinking, and produces one of the most magnificent sequences of poems done in a Western language.

For the second sonnet especially, it might be helpful to mention Wera Ouckama Knoop. She was the daughter of old friends in Munich. Around seventeen, she became ill; it was an incurable glandular disease. She stopped dancing then, and as her body became more heavy and massive, she began to play music, and when her body became still heavier, she began to draw. The sequence touched Rilke. He wants the reader to understand that her figure is not an "anima figure"; she is a real girl.

It was a girl, really—there is a double joy
of poetry and music that she came from—
and I could see her glowing through her spring clothes:
she made a place to sleep inside my ear.

Because she continued to "dance," she overcame greediness. "See, she got up sleeping." Because of her listening as she neared death, a space opened inside him where she could enter his being. "And she slept in me." He didn't feel an obligation to instruct her, or she him. Her calm helped Rilke feel again many twentieth-century experiences: pastures seen from trains, and "every miracle I found in myself." Rilke responds to the flood of perceptions by writing apparent contradictions, as if the Awakener had preserved her from awakening, as if she had awakened still sleeping, as if the instant Eurydice faded back into Hades was exactly the instant she became solid . . . as if true being is not something that can ever be achieved. . . .

The simple facts of Orpheus's story became more and more nourishing to Rilke. Orpheus descended to the underworld and to the dark side of the psyche. Poetry doesn't mean much unless the writer has experienced the dark side. If you arrive at the Grail Castle, you may not ask the question. The dark sexual areas need to be entered. A man's praise of a woman, or hers of a man, become real after the descent to the other world. And the dead are also in that world. The world of the dead—which human beings enter with the help of a medium, or through imagining their own deaths, or through descending into Hades—also underlies true praise.

He can bend down the branches of the willow best
who has experienced the roots of the willow.

Do not entice the dead, Rilke says; simply be confident that they are under your eyelids. He remarks then that those who descend to the dead praise all those inventions that bring the living together: the ring, the water jar, and the bodice clasp.

Rilke suggests that ecstasy, constant good feeling, bliss, hopeful philosophical systems, enlightenment, mean nothing unless the shadow energies have been invited to take part. If people look straight ahead, or look up, and fail to see the Dark Ones standing near, the food will not be nourishing. With that statement he joins Freud's thought for the second time, and joins the thought of Wilhelm Reich, and the whole pre-Christian trust in animals, in sexual life, and dark roots. Rilke early on had written: "My God is dark, and like a webbing made of a hundred roots."

> *Is he from our world? No, his deep nature*
> *grows out of both of the kingdoms.*

James Hillman in *The Dream and the Underworld* reminds us that the soul's ground is below us, in Hades. He says that to the Greeks Hades is moist and nourishing. "Each soul longs to go down." His concern parallels Rilke's concern. Rilke asks: "How do people learn now?" He imagines the three sisters Rejoicing, Longing, and Grief, as if they were sisters in a fairy tale. Rilke thinks that we have exhausted for now the possibility of learning through rejoicing. Longing doesn't pick up much now either, because it is constantly confessing error. "Only Grief still learns."

Rilke doesn't say that we must all praise, or we must all grieve; rather he tries to understand when it is time to do either. Perhaps praising when too young is wrong; perhaps one should be seeing then. After seeing, after listening, after going down, a man or woman could begin to praise. I sometimes think of Emily Dickinson when I read these lines:

> *To praise is the whole thing! A woman who can praise*
> *comes toward us like ore out of the silences*
> *of rock. Her heart, that dies, presses out*
> *for others a wine that is fresh forever.*

One other detail might be helpful for the seventh sonnet. Archaeologists were at work opening tombs. In one untouched tomb the King, the Queen, their family, the servants, the horses, all were lying in the dust. Just over one threshold wrist bones and finger bones were found, and nearby a silver platter, on which one could still see what had been apples and oranges. Rilke found this the most marvelous image conceivable for the poet who gives true praise.

———

The mold in the catacomb of the king
does not suggest that his praising is lies, nor
the fact that the gods cast shadows.

He is one of the servants who does not go away,
who still holds through the doors
of the tomb trays of shining fruit.

One or two notes about the remaining sonnets: the old Roman coffins of stone, which had the lively name "body-eaters" (sarcophagi), survived the fall of Rome. During the Middle Ages, Italian farmers found a use for them. They would knock the ends out and line them up, so they became irrigation canals, carrying water from field to field. Rilke saw that, and it delighted him: water and mourning together.

You stone coffins of the ancient world, I think of you
with joy, you who have never left my feelings,
through which the joyful waters of the days
of Rome flow like some walker's singing.

At Arles he saw a large ancient earth grave; as he watched, butterflies flew out of it.

Or those other graves so open, like the eyes
of a shepherd who wakes up glad,
inside full of silence and pale nettles—
excited butterflies came flying out of them—

The tenth sonnet ends soberly. Even though, helped by our listening, we pass back and forth between the two worlds, traveling swiftly, we still may not know what silence is.

Do ye know what silence is, my friends, or not?
This life that faces both ways
has marked the human face from within.

In this selection you will find only the first ten sonnets. There are forty-five more of them, many of them just as magnificent as the first ten.

When at last the *Sonnets to Orpheus* and the *Duino Elegies* had arrived, Rilke understood that his life's work was over. Despite his neuroticism, his rootlessness, his uncertainty about which class he belonged to, his constant poverty, his confused human obligations, the war, he had done his work. He felt that life had given him a blessing, and in his turn, he laid the *Sonnets* "in the hands of Lou" (Lou Andreas-Salomé).

To me, Rilke stands for toughness, freedom from self-pity, ability to work, whatever one's life situation. He loves spades and hoes and uses images to dig down deeper. His attitude toward the past is to breathe in great art until it fills the lungs. His mode is sacrifice for the sake of that art. His spiritual friend, Rudolf Kassner, told him a sentence he brooded over for years: *"Der Weg von der Innigkeit zur Grösse geht durch das Opfer."* "Going from inwardness to greatness, the road passes through sacrifice." Having arrived at this sentence, we must leave him because we don't know what he sacrificed or what he gained.

In 1922 the *Sonnets* and *Elegies* were done. When not traveling, Rilke lived alone in his last home, the small tower at Muzot, in French-speaking Switzerland. His workroom is there as he left it. In the fall of 1923, he understood that something was wrong with his body, and spent the month of December in the sanatorium of Valmont. He had a rare form of leukemia, but the leukemia was not diagnosed until the late fall of 1926, and there was no cure. He lived in considerable pain throughout December, accompanied only by Nanny Wunderly-Volkart, and died in the very early morning of December 29, 1926. He had already written his epitaph. People all over Europe were reading his poems. The question is, how can a poet whom so many people read keep his privacy? It goes:

> *Rose, oh reiner Widerspruch, Lust,*
> *Niemandes Schlaf zu sein unter soviel*
> *Lidern.*

The difficult word is *Lidern.* This is the word for "eyelids" as well as for the petals of a rose. *Lidern* also makes a pun on *Lieder,* the German word for "songs" or "poems." No single English word forms a resonating box for these three realities. So we could make three versions.

Rose, O pure contradiction, the desire
to be no one's sleep under so many
petals.

Rose, what a contradiction, desire
to be no one's sleep under so many
eyelids.

O rose, you say two things at once, the desire
to be no one's sleep under so many
poems.

Rilke died at fifty-one, and lies buried in the small Swiss church-yard in Raron, with this epitaph above him.

I

Da stieg ein Baum. O reine Übersteigung!
O Orpheus singt! O hoher Baum im Ohr!
Und alles schwieg. Doch selbst in der Verschweigung
ging neuer Anfang, Wink und Wandlung vor.

Tiere aus Stille drangen aus dem klaren
gelösten Wald von Lager und Genist;
und da ergab sich, dass sie nicht aus List
und nicht aus Angst in sich so leise waren,

sondern aus Hören. Brüllen, Schrei, Geröhr
schien klein in ihren Herzen. Und wo eben
kaum eine Hütte war, dies zu empfangen,

ein Unterschlupf aus dunkelstem Verlangen
mit einem Zugang, dessen Pfosten beben,—
da schufst du ihnen Tempel im Gehör.

———

I

A tree rising. What a pure growing!
Orpheus is singing! A tree inside the ear!
Silence, silence. Yet new buildings,
signals, and changes went on in the silence.

Animals created by silence came forward from the clear
and relaxed forest where their lairs were,
and it turned out the reason they were so full of silence
was not cunning, and not terror,

it was listening. Growling, yelping, grunting now
seemed all nonsense to them. And where before
there was hardly a shed where this listening could go,

a rough shelter put up out of brushy longings,
with an entrance gate whose poles were wobbly,
you created a temple for them deep inside their ears.

II

Und fast ein Mädchen wars und ging hervor
aus diesem einigen Glück von Sang und Leier
und glänzte klar durch ihre Frühlingsschleier
und machte sich ein Bett in meinem Ohr.

Und schlief in mir. Und alles war ihr Schlaf.
Die Bäume, die ich je bewundert, diese
fühlbare Ferne, die gefühlte Wiese
und jedes Staunen, das mich selbst betraf.

Sie schlief die Welt. Singender Gott, wie hast
du sie vollendet, dass sie nicht begehrte,
erst wach zu sein? Sieh, sie erstand und schlief.

Wo ist ihr Tod? O, wirst du dies Motiv
erfinden noch, eh sich dein Lied verzehrte?—
Wo sinkt sie hin aus mir? . . . Ein Mädchen fast. . . .

II

It was a girl, really—there is a double joy
of poetry and music that she came from—
and I could see her glowing through her spring clothes:
she made a place to sleep inside my ear.

And she slept in me. Her sleep was everything.
The trees I'd always loved, those distances that we
can almost touch, the pastures I felt so much,
and every miracle I found in myself.

She was sleeping it all. Wild Singing God,
how did you do it so that she had no desire at all
to be awake? See, she got up sleeping.

And when will she die? And you want to find this out,
also, even before your poem fades?
Where is she going to, as she sinks away . . . a girl really . . .

III

Ein Gott vermags. Wie aber, sag mir, soll
ein Mann ihm folgen durch die schmale Leier?
Sein Sinn ist Zwiespalt. An der Kreuzung zweier
Herzwege steht kein Tempel für Apoll.

Gesang, wie du ihn lehrst, ist nicht Begehr,
nicht Werbung um ein endlich noch Erreichtes;
Gesang ist Dasein. Für den Gott ein Leichtes.
Wann aber sind wir? Und wann wendet er

an unser Sein die Erde und die Sterne?
Dies ists nicht, Jüngling, dass du liebst, wenn auch
die Stimme dann den Mund dir aufstösst,—lerne

vergessen, dass du aufsangst. Das verrinnt.
In Wahrheit singen, ist ein andrer Hauch.
Ein Hauch um nichts. Ein Wehn im Gott. Ein Wind.

III

A god can do it. But tell me, how can a man
follow his narrow road through the strings?
A man is split. And where two roads intersect
inside us, no one has built the Singer's Temple.

Writing poetry as we learn from you is not desiring,
not wanting something that can ever be achieved.
To write poetry is to be alive. For a god that's easy.
When, however, are we really alive? And when does he

turn the earth and the stars so they face us?
Yes, you are young, and you love, and the voice
forces your mouth open—that is lovely, but learn

to forget that breaking into song. It doesn't last,
Real singing is a different movement of air.
Air moving around nothing. A breathing in a god. A wind.

IV

O ihr Zärtlichen, tretet zuweilen
in den Atem, der euch nicht meint,
lasst ihn an eueren Wangen sich teilen
hinter euch zittert er, wieder vereint.

O ihr Seligen, o ihr Heilen,
die ihr der Anfang der Herzen scheint.
Bogen der Pfeile und Ziele von Pfeilen,
ewiger glänzt euer Lächeln verweint.

Fürchtet euch nicht zu leiden, die Schwere,
gebt sie zurück an der Erde Gewicht;
schwer sind die Berge, schwer sind die Meere.

Selbst die als Kinder ihr pflanztet, die Bäume,
wurden zu schwer längst; ihr trüget sie nicht.
Aber die Lüfte . . . aber die Räume . . .

IV

O you lovers that are so gentle, step occasionally
into the breath of the sufferers not meant for you,
let it be parted by your cheeks,
it will tremble, joined again, behind you.

You have been chosen, you are sound and whole,
you are like the very first beat of the heart,
you are the bow that shoots the arrows, and also their target,
in tears your smile would glow forever.

Do not be afraid to suffer, give
the heaviness back to the weight of the earth;
mountains are heavy, seas are heavy.

Even those trees you planted as children
became too heavy long ago—you couldn't carry them now.
But you can carry the winds . . . and the open spaces . . .

V

Errichtet keinen Denkstein. Lasst die Rose
nur jedes Jahr zu seinen Gunsten blühn.
Denn Orpheus ists. Seine Metamorphose
in dem und dem. Wir sollen uns nicht mühn

um andre Namen. Ein für alle Male
ists Orpheus, wenn es singt. Er kommt und geht.
Ists nicht schon viel, wenn er die Rosenschale
um ein paar Tage manchmal übersteht?

O wie er schwinden muss, dass ihrs begrifft!
Und wenn ihm selbst auch bangte, dass er schwände.
Indem sein Wort das Hiersein übertrifft,

ist er schon dort, wohin ihrs nicht begleitet.
Der Leier Gitter zwängt ihm nicht die Hände.
Und er gehorcht, indem er überschreitet.

V

Don't bother about a stone. Let the rose simply
bloom each year in his memory.
The rose is Orpheus. He takes different shapes
in this and that. There's no need to worry

about all those names. Once and for all,
if there is poetry, Orpheus is there. He comes and goes.
Isn't it already a lot that he sometimes survives
by a few days the rose leaves in the bowl?

Yes, and he has to go, or you won't understand!
Even though he himself is afraid he might disappear forever!
The instant his poem rises above day-by-day things,

he is already in a place where you cannot follow him.
The strings of the lyre do not entangle his hands.
And he obeys in exactly the instant he steps over.

VI

Ist er ein Hiesiger? Nein, aus beiden
Reichen erwuchs seine weite Natur.
Kundiger böge die Zweige der Weiden,
wer die Wurzeln der Weiden erfuhr.

Geht ihr zu Bette, so lasst auf dem Tische
Brot nicht und Milch nicht; die Toten ziehts—.
Aber er, der Beschwörende, mische
unter der Milde des Augenlids

ihre Erscheinung in alles Geschaute;
und der Zauber von Erdrauch und Raute
sei ihm so wahr wie der klarste Bezug.

Nichts kann das gültige Bild ihm verschlimmern;
sei es aus Gräbern, sei es aus Zimmern,
rühme er Fingerring, Spange und Krug.

VI

Is he from our world? No, his deep nature
grows out of both of the kingdoms.
He can bend down the branches of the willow best
who has experienced the roots of the willow.

When you go to bed, do not leave bread
behind on the table, or milk; they will entice the dead.
But Orpheus, a shaman, infuses their spirits
into everything that can be seen

beneath the quietness of the closed eyes;
and the magic meaning of rue and smokeherb
is as clear to him as the sharpest logic.

Nothing can blur the real image for him;
whether drawn from tombs or from our houses,
he praises the ring, the clasp, and the water jar!

VII

Rühmen, das ists! Ein zum Rühmen Bestellter,
ging er hervor wie das Erz aus des Steins
Schweigen. Sein Herz, o vergängliche Kelter
eines den Menschen unendlichen Weins.

Nie versagt ihm die Stimme am Staube,
wenn ihn das göttliche Beispiel ergreift.
Alles wird Weinberg, alles wird Traube,
in seinem fühlenden Süden gereift.

Nicht in den Grüften der Könige Moder
straft ihm die Rühmung Lügen, oder
dass von den Göttern ein Schatten fällt.

Es ist einer der bleibenden Boten,
der noch weit in die Türen der Toten
Schalen mit rühmlichen Früchten hält.

VII

To praise is the whole thing! A man who can praise
comes toward us like ore out of the silences
of rock. His heart, that dies, presses out
for others a wine that is fresh forever.

When the god's energy takes hold of him,
his voice never collapses in the dust.
Everything turns to vineyards, everything turns to grapes,
made ready for harvest by his powerful south.

The mold in the catacomb of the king
does not suggest that his praising is lies, nor
the fact that the gods cast shadows.

He is one of the servants who does not go away,
who still holds through the doors
of the tomb trays of shining fruit.

VIII

Nur im Raum der Rühmung darf die Klage
gehn, die Nymphe des geweinten Quells,
wachend über unserm Niederschlage,
dass er klar sei an demselben Fels,

der die Tore trägt und die Altäre.—
Sieh, um ihre stillen Schultern früht
das Gefühl, dass sie die jüngste wäre
unter den Geschwistern im Gemüt.

Jubel weiss, und Sehnsucht ist geständig,—
nur die Klage lernt noch; mädchenhändig
zählt sie nächtelang das alte Schlimme.

Aber plötzlich, schräg und ungeübt,
hält sie doch ein Sternbild unsrer Stimme
in den Himmel, den ihr Hauch nicht trübt.

VIII

Where praise already is is the only place Grief
ought to go, that water spirit of the pools of tears;
she watches over our defeats to make sure
the water rises clear from the same rock

that holds up the huge doors and the altars.
You can see, around her motionless shoulders, a feeling
dawns—we sense more and more that she
is the youngest of the three sisters we have inside.

Rejoicing has lost her doubts, and Longing broods on her error,
Only Grief still learns: she spends the whole night
counting up our evil inheritance with her small hands.

She is awkward, but all at once
she makes our voice rise, sideways, like a constellation
into the sky, not troubled by her breath.

I X

Nur wer die Leier schon hob
auch unter Schatten,
darf das unendliche Lob
ahnend erstatten.

Nur wer mit Toten vom Mohn
ass, von dem ihren,
wird nicht den leisesten Ton
wieder verlieren.

Mag auch die Spieglung im Teich
Oft uns verschwimmen:
Wisse das Bild.

Erst in dem Doppelbereich
werden die Stimmen
ewig und mild.

IX

Only the man who has raised his strings
among the dark ghosts also
should feel his way toward
the endless praise.

Only he who has eaten poppy
with the dead, from their poppy,
will never lose even
his most delicate sound.

Even though images in the pool
seem so blurry:
grasp the main thing.

Only in the double kingdom, there
alone, will voices become
undying and tender.

X

Euch, die ihr nie mein Gefühl verliesst,
grüss ich, antikische Sarkophage,
die das fröhliche Wasser römischer Tage
als ein wandelndes Lied durchfliesst.

Oder jene so offenen, wie das Aug
eines frohen erwachenden Hirten,
—innen voll Stille und Bienensaug—
denen entzückte Falter entschwirrten;

alle, die man dem Zweifel entreisst,
grüss ich, die wiedergeöffneten Munde,
die schon wussten, was schweigen heisst.

Wissen wirs, Freunde, wissen wirs nicht?
Beides bildet die zögernde Stunde
in dem menschlichen Angesicht.

X

You stone coffins of the ancient world, I think of you
with joy, you who have never left my feelings,
through which the joyful waters of the days
of Rome flow like some walker's singing.

Or those other graves so open, like the eyes
of a shepherd who wakes up glad,
inside full of silence and pale nettles—
excited butterflies came flying out of them—

Now I turn joyfully to everything that has been torn
away from doubt, the mouths open again,
after having known what silence is.

Do we know what silence is, my friends, or not?
This life that faces both ways
has marked the human face from within.

Indexes

Index of Titles in German

Index of Titles in English

Index of First Lines in German

Index of First Lines in English